A Path of Encounter

ALSO BY JON MCALICE

Engaged Community: The Challenge of Self-Governance in Waldorf Education

A PATH OF

ENCOUNTER

---

meditation,
practice,
and the
art of sensing

Jon McAlice

Lindisfarne | 2015

Published by
LINDISFARNE BOOKS
An imprint of Anthroposophic Press, Inc.
610 Main Street, Great Barrington, Massachusetts 01230
www.steinerbooks.org

Print ISBN: 978-1-58420-188-5
eBook ISBN: 978-1-58420-189-2

Printed in the United States of America.

CONTENTS

Foreword

This book was written in response to a question I have had in recent years. It arose in connection with a feeling of unease experienced when in dialogue with others concerning the inner path of development described by Rudolf Steiner. I found that many of the things I have come to understand as being essential to this path were not present in others' depictions of anthroposophical practice. It has often seemed to me that these depictions expressed an interpretive approach to Steiner's work rooted in a rather conventional and thus general understanding of contemplative and meditative practices. Where was the radical uniqueness and freely responsive intentionality so apparent in Steiner's own life and work? And I found myself grappling ever more intensely with the question: What does anthroposophy look like when experienced through Rudolf Steiner's eyes?

A Path of Encounter is thus a first attempt to voice an understanding of Steiner "from the inside out." It is personal.

For that I make no apologies. Others can do it their ways; I can only do it mine. Whatever limitations are to be found in the presentation are my own, not Steiner's.

Over the last decades Steiner's work, as it comes to expression in such areas as education, farming, medicine, etc., has been rediscovered and received a good deal of positive attention. Not so Steiner himself. He remains an enigma, for the most part. Many of those who are so ready to embrace the fruits of his work are explicitly less eager to consider the path upon which they arose. Even some of the more prominent figures in the anthroposophical movement have voiced the need to move past Steiner and bring anthroposophy into the modern world.

While this may be true in regard to whatever in Steiner's work is defined by the historical context in which he lived, it has no validity in regard to the path of inner schooling he described. Only one who has progressed further along this path than Rudolf Steiner did would be justified in making such a statement, but would have no need to do so.

On the other side of the aisle sit those who would deify Rudolf Steiner and have others do the same. This is one of the few things Steiner asked his listeners not to do. The challenge is to understand, not worship.

I have met many people who have helped me to see aspects of Steiner's path that I do not think I would have discovered on my own. Some of them, like Elena Zuccoli, experienced Steiner personally. Others, like Ernst-Michael Kranich, dedicated their lives to mastering specific aspects of Steiner's teachings. Nana Goebel and Bernd Ruf, among others, have worked tirelessly to bring the fruits of this work to those most in need. To all of them, my deepest gratitude.

This book would not have been possible without the generosity of a number of people. John Gouldthorpe, Gary Lachmann, and Aksel Hugo all took time to read the manuscript thoroughly and offer suggestions. Beth and Eric have been instrumental in keeping me moving. Chris Bamford is the most gentle, supportive editor one could hope for. I feel very fortunate to have been able to work with all of these individuals.

Heinz Zimmermann, a teacher, scholar and thinker introduced me both to the majesty of the Swiss mountains and to the delicate wonder of Rudolf Steiner's path of modern initiation with its unique blend of earnestness and Schillerian playfulness. Since his presence is to be felt whenever I tackle a project, I thought I would let him get a word in at the beginning:

> The uniqueness of this path is its point of departure: the intentional development of the soul capacity in which we are most awake, the capacity of thinking. The transformation and spiritualization of thinking is the beginning of the path. This does not exclude feeling and willing, something that has often been misunderstood, but instead raises these to a higher, more conscious level. All aspects of consciousness must today be intentionally sculpted and individualized. This can only happen through experiencing them. In this way it is possible for ideas to become ideals that we learn to love and that move us deeply enough that they can become actions.

This is the challenge of our time. We tend to know much and do little. For Steiner, this dilemma was not merely a question of what we think, but, more important, how we think it. The spiritualization of thinking awakens to life what otherwise is trapped in a web of reflected uncertainty and doubt. It enables individual consciousness to become a willing participant in the shaping of a more humane future built on an engaged selflessness able to embrace the needs of the other as its own.

JON MCALICE
Ghent, New York
November 2014

I. A Different Path

Two roads diverged in a yellow wood
And sorry I could not travel both
And be one traveller, long I stood...

Robert Frost

Each time we turn around, in every moment of every day, we are confronted with the miracle of our existence. The song of the birds in the morning heralds the coming of spring although the snow still lies thick in the garden and the paths are frozen hard as stone. The joy ringing in a child's laughter, the earnestness with which a boy struggles to finger the melody he hears so well within, the timelessness of a good conversation—all lead us beyond the limitations of our preoccupied selves into a fleeting encounter with something greater, more noble, a mysterious expanse of inestimable beauty and potential. In such moments, if we don't let them slip away unnoticed, it is possible to feel a sense of homecoming, to sense that the feelings stirred by such encounters resonate with something that lies at the very core of our selves. This experience points toward something in us that is at once concrete and transcendent, completely rooted in the present yet graced by eternity. If I stop to ponder this experience, I find myself faced with a riddle: the riddle of my own being. The encounter with this riddle is to be taken seriously. It is perhaps the most significant encounter you can have in life.

What is it in this encounter that is so special? In such moments, if you are awake to them, you find yourself in the presence of something greater: something worth striving towards. The recognition of the miraculous, the sublimely beautiful, the transcendentally joyous is an act of consciousness that resonates with the miraculous, the sublime, the transcendent nature of our own beingness. This is also true of moments of empathy or compassion. Our capacity to experience the joy or sorrow of another being as though it were our own belies the notion that human consciousness is trapped within a web of its own weaving, ever separate from the world it longs to know. Our consciousness reaches beyond the purely sense perceptible of the material world, plunging into the in-between, the realm of relationships, the invisible space in which everything is connected, into the space in which the presence of the spirit is manifest.

There is deep need today to find a new, experienced connection to the spirit. As a global community, we are facing challenges that require of us practiced responses born of a sense of living connectedness to the world, to one another and to ourselves. Only a consciousness that can embrace the other as oneself, that knows the world from within and that can illuminate actions born of empathetic participation and engagement can begin to fathom the enormity of what faces us as human beings.

Participatory consciousness does not develop of its own accord. Although the seeds of such a consciousness are planted deep within the spiritual reality of human existence, they will only grow if each one of us chooses to nurture them. Their growth is dependent on individual intentionality. Others may call my attention to their existence, but only I can enable them to unfold, blossom and bear fruit within me and through me in the world.

The cultivation of these seeds of conscious connectedness is possible through inner discipline and intentional practice. In this sense, we can speak of spiritual discipline or spiritual practice. Today each of us who discovers within himself or herself an obligation to nurture these inner seeds of growth and change is called upon to find the practice or discipline that is right for him or for her. The path that each one of us travels will, of necessity, be one's own.

That said, no serious seeker will disregard the experiences of those who have embarked on this journey before. There is a long and rich tradition of spiritual practices. Each traditional culture has such a path. Over the course of the last hundred years, many of these paths have been documented by Western scholars and made available to the general public. Aspects of some of them have become part of modern culture. It is, for instance, not uncommon to hear someone speak of "good parking space karma" or "good taxi karma." Meditation practices once unique to Tibetan monks are now common fare in corporate trainings. What we often forget is that these ideas and practices were once embedded in rich cultural contexts and accompanied by strict discipline and intense training. The self-fulfillment rhetoric that accompanies them in our pluralistic society dissociates them from both the cultural and moral context within which they could be most fruitful.

Although this is most evident with those practices firmly rooted in traditional cultures, it is also apparent with more modern spiritual paths. One of these is anthroposophy, the spiritual practices that arose out of the path taken by the Austrian teacher and practitioner Rudolf Steiner. One of the most misunderstood figures in Western culture, Rudolf Steiner is viewed skeptically by scientists and spiritualists alike.

For the former, he is too "out there" with his talk of angels and spirit beings; for the latter, his complex conceptual approach lacks the kind of spontaneity and intuitive simplicity one expects in a mystic. Instead of flowing robes and a colorful lifestyle, you get black frockcoats and outer conventionality; instead of skeptical argumentation based on Kantian principles, you get spiritual imaginations rooted in an epistemology of conceptual immediacy. As he would say with some impatience toward the end of his life, those who nodded most ardently during his lectures understood nothing of what he was saying, and those who could understand weren't listening. And nothing was more important to him than to be understood: not revered or worshipped, just understood.

Rudolf Steiner died in 1925. He left an enormous body

of work comprising some 6000 lecture transcripts and 30 volumes of books and articles. The majority of the lectures and writings date from between 1900 and his death. In those 25 years, he not only described a path of inner schooling for the modern seeker, he also trod that path and articulated the insights that he gained upon the way. This body of knowledge—the teachings of anthroposophy— revolves around a new understanding of the human being, the role of human consciousness in cosmic evolution and the spiritual nature of human individuality. It is at once unique and at the same time deeply indebted to the great teachers of the past.

Today, there is a danger that anthroposophy is losing its identity as a spiritual practice. As the various spiritual paths become increasingly a part of popular culture, the tendency to blur the differences between them increases also. This is unfortunate. Different paths are there for a reason. Each one speaks to the human soul in a unique way. Each has its own language, its own voice. It is the context within which they are spoken that gives the words their meaning. Taken out of context, they lose their richness and, to a great extent, their magic. Spirit does not mean the same in every context.

Rudolf Steiner was an anomaly among modern spiritual seekers. His own inner path led him to recognize aspects of the soul's development of which others took no notice. Thus, the path he described in his work, although intimately related to other paths of inner development, has aspects that are not to be found anywhere else. Recognizing and understanding these enable one to see anthroposophy in relation to other paths, and to honor its essential differences.

We have become somewhat skittish when it comes to addressing differences. Things appear to flow more smoothly when we focus on commonalities. There is a very real longing to grasp the oneness of the world. A consciousness of the differences that are present seems to disturb the tentative togetherness we hope to feel. Pointing out differences often brings a critical edge into discussions that many experience as painful. In the final analysis, we are all the same, aren't we? Human beings are human beings. The differences between us pale in contrast to what we have in common.

Although such a train of thought may serve to calm one's own nagging questions, in life the differences are what make the difference. Not all roads lead to the same destination. The acorn that falls in the forest will have a different future than the one that falls in a field. Although in theory every person could be your friend, it is the particular friends you have that give your life its essential flavor.

To understand life, you must come to a deep appreciation of differences, of the unique, the specifically essential. Commonality is something we achieve thanks to and in spite of our differences.

What is true in life is also true, perhaps even more so, in matters of the spirit.

Rudolf Steiner's path, the path we know today as anthroposophy, has aspects that are unique, and which set it apart from other spiritual paths just as the Zen path differs from the path of Christian mystic, or as the path of a Mongolian shaman differs from that of a Hindu yogi. Recognizing these differences helps us to understand more fully the nature and value of each of these paths, whereas simply mixing elements from all of them into a generalized path to spirituality robs each of them of its own identity, the source of its power.

In the following, I have tried to highlight certain essential aspects of the path Rudolf Steiner described. I have done so with some hesitation, knowing full well that there are others with a richer understanding of these matters than I possess. Having walked this path for close to 30 years, I find that I am less certain of many of its nuances than I was when I began. It is a path that grows increasingly complex and laden with potential the further one progresses.

A number of events over the course of the last decade or so have pushed me to tackle this project. One occurred soon after I had moved back to America with my family after working at the Goetheanum in Dornach, Switzerland, the center of the international anthroposophical movement. We left Switzerland in the winter of 2000 and arrived in California in late August. Soon after, I was asked by a local Waldorf school to host a series of evening discussions for parents around the question: What is anthroposophy? On the first evening I found myself in a circle of about 20 people. As we went around introducing ourselves, it became apparent that most in the circle had a connection to Zen Buddhism. This was not surprising in Marin County. Just ten miles to the south is Green Gulch Farm, one of the centers that grew up around the teachings of Shunryu Suzuki Roshi. When I asked if anyone had any specific question they would like to ask before we began, one father spoke up, saying: "I have been a parent in a Waldorf school for almost 15 years now. Something puzzles me. When I ask the teachers questions, they always have wonderful, spiritually interesting answers. In fact, they seem to have such answers for almost everything. But what I have yet to learn is what their practice is. In Zen, there are things we do every day. What is the practice of anthroposophy?"

What is the practice of anthroposophy? Today, some 14 years later, this question is as present for me as it was for all of us that autumn evening. Is anthroposophy but a body of revealed spiritual knowledge? Or is it a discipline, a path toward spiritual understanding? If it is the latter, as this father so rightly noted, there must be a practice, and how does this practice or discipline differ from other practices?

Discipline means different things in different cultures. It appears in the English language in the 13th century by way of old French and Latin. At that time it meant the instruction given to a disciple, connoting the order necessary for instruction. Over the centuries, the word has taken on different connotations. The first definition in the 2005 edition of the Oxford American Dictionary is: "1) the practice of training people to obey rules or a code of behavior, using punishment to correct disobedience." Common usage applies this definition to the classroom and the military. Although the use of the word in conjunction with spiritual development is, of course, not unknown in the English language, it does demand overcoming certain prejudices. Spiritual discipline must come from within, not from without. In terms of spiritual development, discipline indicates the activities an individual practices in order to refine the faculties of his or her soul.

Each culture has its own words to describe this process; I know of no traditional culture from which it is absent. Wherever the human being has come to experience the riddle of the inner life of the soul, practices have evolved that support the attainment of something higher within. In Japanese, for instance, the word to describe this path is *tanren*, a word also used to denote one step in the forging of fine blades. A *katana*, the sword of the Samurai, is forged in this manner, as are the blades found in Japanese woodworking tools. If you ever have the opportunity to use such blades, do so. They are quite different from Western tools. Not only are they formed differently, they are held differently and they cut differently. The process of forging that the term tanren refers to is one in which the steel is heated, folded over onto itself, then cooled in water. This folding is repeated 12 to 14 times, purifying the steel of all its impurities. In the schools of Japanese martial arts, most notably karate and aikido, tanren translates as "spirit-forging." The discipline of the martial art cleanses the spirit of its impurities.

Anthroposophy is also a path of purification. The tools you take to hand are gentler than the hammer upon the anvil. You can't hammer your way to a conscious experience of the spirit. On the other hand, the resistance you meet within yourself can be as unbending as cold steel. It needs to be warmed, to become pliable and slowly reshaped. As with the forging of the steel, this is a process of refining. We become increasingly sensitive to the finer things in life, the details, the nuances. We become aware of what is not immediately apparent.

Thus, the discipline that lies at the heart of anthroposophy revolves around practices of inner refinement that enable the individual soul to free itself of the limitations brought about by its dependence on the body and become more attuned to the presence of the spirit both within and around it. What are these practices?

In the following chapters some of them, I hope, will become apparent, as will the experiences from which they arose.

II. A Spiritual Anthropology

What spirit is, my friend, cannot be described, drawn, painted—but it can be felt, it expresses itself through thoughts, movements, through striving, force and effect. In the corporeal world we distinguish spirit from the body and attribute to spirit what ensouls the body down to its elements, what holds life within it and awakens life, what attracts forces and reproduces forces. Hence in the oldest languages, spirit was the expression for invisible, striving might ...

Johann Gottfried Herder

Like many modern spiritual teachers, Rudolf Steiner grew up in a non-religious environment. His childhood was spent in train stations on the fringes of the Austrian-Hungarian empire. Growing up, he was equally impressed by both the majesty of the great locomotives that passed through the stations and the unspoiled nature that surrounded the small towns to which his father was sent. According to his own accounts, as a child, he was quite open for experiences of a supersensory nature. He mentions certain spiritual encounters that he experienced in spite of the lack of openness for such things in his immediate surroundings. One was the encounter with the soul of his dead aunt that took place before word had reached the family of her suicide. In his autobiography, he writes also of the deep impression the services in the local church made upon him, services that he attended alone.

Also in his autobiography, he writes of an experience that would prove to play a central role in his later work. It took place when he was nine years old. He discovered a geometry book in his teacher's study and asked to borrow it. He plunged himself into the study of geometry, struggling with the laws of triangles, the riddle of parallel lines, the theorem of Pythagoras:

> I derived a deep feeling of contentment from the fact that one could live with the soul in building forms that are seen wholly inwardly, independent of the outer senses. I found consolation for the unrest caused by so many unanswered questions. The ability to grasp something purely through the spirit brought me an inner joy. I realized that I first knew true happiness through geometry.[1]

These lines, written when Steiner was nearing the end of his life, are key to understanding his approach to spiritual development.

Although modern science tends to negate the notion of the soul as an entity, throughout the 19th century the concept of the soul was very much alive both in religious and in scientific circles. The question was not whether the human being has a soul, but concerned rather the nature of

---

1   Rudolf Steiner, *Autobiography*, p. 9

the soul. The soul was an experience. No one questioned whether or not the experience of soul was real. For the young Steiner, the recognition of the spiritual dimensions of the inner life of the soul was a touchstone in his awakening.

Set across from his youthful discoveries concerning the presence of the spiritual in the soul, were the emergent scientific explanations of the nature of the soul. In keeping with the axiomatic dualism that underlay contemporary scientific inquiry, the soul was coming to be seen as an epiphenomenon brought about by then yet to be identified biological functions. There was no room for spiritual experience within these parameters.

This approach to understanding the human being's experience of consciousness is as much a part of our modern lives as are Google and Apple. It has had a deep impact on how we think about ourselves and about our relation to the world around us. It colors the way we think about our own experiences of the spiritual, constantly calling into question our own spiritual nature.

According to his own accounts, Rudolf Steiner had a strong sense of the presence of the spiritual during his childhood. He found no way to share this experience and yet was certain of its validity. This isolated him from his surroundings. He was the "stranger in the village." His experience was of both the "visible" and the "invisible," the sense-perceptible and the supersensible. Those around him knew only of the visible world the mind was able to grasp through the senses. He experienced the sense world as the outer expression of a spiritual presence. This presence of the spiritual gave the sense world meaning and beauty.

Yet, for the child, it was something that could only be experienced, not known and understood. In the local church, he could feel the sublime power of the sacrament, the act of ushering the invisible into the world of the visible, but he had not yet found a way to make sense of it.

Until his experience with the purely spiritual nature of geometrical thinking.

Looking back on this experience, the 63-year-old Steiner would write:

> I must acknowledge that my relationship to geometry was the beginning of a view that took shape gradually within me. During childhood it lived in me more or less unconsciously; by my twentieth year it had assumed a definite, fully conscious form. I would have said that the objects and events seen by the senses exist in space, the space outside the human being; but a kind of soul-space exists within as the setting for spiritual beings and events. I could not see anything in thoughts that was like the pictures we form of things; rather they were revelations of a spiritual world on the stage of the soul.[2]

In struggling with the lawfulness of geometrical relationships, the nine-year-old boy experienced something in thinking that would accompany him the rest of his life. It was not simply a matter of learning geometry, remembering the axioms and constructing proofs. Many youngsters

2   Ibid.

are forced through this exercise at some point in life. What Steiner discovered in doing this seeded an understanding of the role of thinking within the soul. As a result, his relationship to thinking changed. It became an experienced space to be explored and mastered. He did thinking the way others do dance or farming or write poetry. He became a connoisseur of thought, tasting, as it were, the movements and gestures of thoughts as they unfolded and blossomed. Immersed in the dynamic flow of living ideas, he grasped with certainty the reality of the spiritual world, a world that was as real for him as the physical world around him.

This relationship to the thinking soul was the center of Rudolf Steiner's life for many years. He did well enough in school to earn a scholarship to the Technical Institute in Vienna, where he studied physics and mathematics, while at the same time working his way through the writings of Immanuel Kant and his successors. At this time, he felt it "his duty to discover the truth through philosophy."[3] His experiences of the spiritual remained for the most part private. The few attempts he made to share these with others were met with a lack of understanding.

Already at this time, Steiner had found a relationship to the spiritual that diverged from that of his contemporaries. He spoke of his experiences with a mathematical clarity and philosophical certainty that, while acceptable when discussing problems of physics or epistemology, met with skepticism when he turned to questions of the spirit. The prevalent belief was that the spiritual lay beyond the

_____

3   Ibid., p. 28

boundaries of what could be grasped by thought. This was, however, not Steiner's experience. He had realized that thinking knew no absolute boundaries. It could lead one beyond the conceptual relationships dictated by the world of sense perceptible objects. But within the circle of scholars and artists with whom he communed in Vienna and later in Weimar, he was alone in this view. He ceased trying to share his experiences of the spiritual. Instead he focused on his studies and, later, on his work as editor of the German poet and thinker Johann Wolfgang von Goethe's scientific writings.

He was 20 years old when he was recommended for this job by one of his professors, Karl Julius Schroer, a man who had made a genuine and lasting impression on him. Through him, Steiner gained a deep appreciation of Goethe's work. During the period of his acquaintanceship with Schroer, Steiner had conducted an intense private study of optics, then anatomy and morphology. He had become acutely aware of the problems of a de-humanized science, in which the individual can only be the observer, never a participant in the natural world; in which human presence can only disturb, never enhance nature. Through such an approach humans can learn to manipulate the parts, but never understand the whole. For Steiner, this view was based on an inadequate understanding of human consciousness, focusing only on an unfounded exaggeration of both the value and the limitations of human reason. His own studies convinced him that Goethe's approach to science led to a true understanding of phenomena, not merely to theoretical explanations about them. Based on Steiner's interest and insight into Goethe's work, Schroer recommended him to edit Goethe's scientific writings. Just nine months after accepting the position, Steiner had completed the first of what would eventually become four volumes. It was his first major literary endeavor.

The encounter with Goethe's work and the intense study of his scientific method mark a turning point for Rudolf Steiner. Although he did not attempt to recreate Goethe's observations, he did live into Goethe's descriptions of his experiments and musings, and in doing so was able to cast light on the phenomenological method that lay at the foundation of Goethe's discoveries. Through this process he not only became aware of, but was able to articulate in detail, a scientific approach that through the inner re-creation of the outer phenomenon could lead to an ever-deeper understanding of the living forces at work in the latter. By living into Goethe's way of thinking, he became able to bear witness to what would become known as the Goethean method.

Goethe described his approach as a delicate empiricism, a gentle, rigorous examination of the phenomenon, led by the question: If it could speak, what would it say about itself? He approached nature with a gesture of reverence, the feeling of awe you might experience when in the presence of the divine. This restrained him from applying any preconceived theoretical constructs to the objects of his observations. He observed, re-imagined and listened within to what they might reveal of themselves. He practiced a patient science that led him step by step to an intuitive understanding of the natural world, to a conceptual experience of the "thing in itself."

This was especially true in Goethe's approach to understanding the living world. No single perceptual experience of a plant can reveal the totality of the plant's nature. This unfolds over time. You can gain a sense of the plant if you observe it at various stages of its growth, forming an exact inner picture of what you observe, an exact sensory imagination, and then bring these inner re-creations into relation with one another. By doing so, you begin to gain a sense of that plant as something that extends beyond any one stage, something that brings itself to full expression in re-forming itself sequentially. You begin to intuit the plant, the chicory or the dandelion, as something that embraces all the various stages, and is expressed fully in none. For Goethe, only this supra-sensory, never (yet always) seen, formative reality, the generative concept, could give true insight into the nature of the living world.

Over the course of many years, Goethe's study of the plant world led him to the point where he could speak of the archetypal plant, the conceptual gesture of plantness that brings itself to such a multitude of expressions as we find spread throughout the plant world. In the now famous conversation with Schiller, during which Goethe shared his discovery with his friend, Schiller pointed out to him that his notion of the archetypal plant was an idea, a theoretical construct abstracted from nature. Goethe is said to have replied, "How wonderful that I have ideas without knowing it, and am able to see them with my very own eyes!"[4]

Steiner also wrote about this conversation in his auto-biography, noting: "I felt that I had come to understand these words of Goethe; to me they meant inner peace after a long struggle."[5] For Steiner, Goethe became a spiritual comrade, a friendly presence in this period of loneliness. His impact on Steiner's future path is immense. Through Goethe, Steiner became acquainted with an approach to knowledge that made it possible for him to articulate his own experience and develop a path of inner schooling that would lead to a conscious, intentional exploration of the nature of spiritual reality.

The first challenge he faced, however, was to lay the epistemological groundwork for Goethe's way of thinking. Goethe's experience of the sensory-suprasensory idea, the generative concept of organic wholeness in the natural world, found no resonance in the then contemporary understanding of how a human being knows the world. Steiner found himself forced to create the epistemological underpinnings of an understanding of Goethe's way of knowing. Drawing on his own experience and his insight into Goethe's work, he drafted the first of his epistemological studies, *Goethe's Way of Knowing*. This was published in 1886, just two years after the first volumes of Goethe's scientific writings went to press, and would be followed by *Truth and Science* (1890) and, finally, *The Philosophy of Freedom* (1893).

---

4   Quoted from Suchankte, 2009.
5   Rudolf Steiner, *Autobiography*, p. 49

No approach to anthroposophy that does not find its philosophical or epistemological roots in the understanding of thinking and the idea of freedom that Steiner develops in the course of these three studies can begin to do justice to the spiritual path that grew out of them. Together they mark a paradigmatic shift in the understanding of human consciousness and the role it plays in cosmic evolution.

The last of the three, *The Philosophy of Freedom* or, the English title Steiner suggested, *The Philosophy of Spiritual Activity*, is purely Steiner, and can be seen as the beginning of what would become a 30-year battle with the narrow-mindedness of the academic and scientific world. In contrast to *Truth and Science*, Rudolf Steiner's doctoral dissertation, which was published in book form in 1890, his *Philosophy of Freedom* is not an epistemological study in the classical sense of the word. He addressed the epistemological questions in his dissertation, focusing on the work of Immanuel Kant and Johann Gottlieb Fichte. In *The Philosophy of Freedom*, he develops a practice of knowing that leads to action born of insight and lays the groundwork for what Karl-Martin Dietz among others has termed an anthropology of the higher self (Dietz, et al., 1994).

It is impossible to overestimate the significance of this book for Steiner's work. The only revisions he made to what he had written in his early 30s appeared in the new edition published in 1918. In the foreword, he noted that the book was "practically unaltered in all its essentials."[6]

---

6   Although this statement may be true in regard to the content of the book, it does not reflect the difference in tone between the first

He made additions to certain chapters and rewrote some passages, in which he felt he had "expressed himself clumsily." He changed nothing of the essence, although in the ensuing years, he had published a large number of works describing the results of his spiritual research. *The Philosophy of Freedom* contains nothing of this sort.

Its focus is exclusively the human soul.

In a letter to Rosa Mayreder, Steiner's free-thinking comrade from his days in Vienna, he narrows this focus even more:

> I don't try to teach: I narrate my inner experiences. I tell the story the way I have lived it. Everything in the book is personal. The form of the thoughts as well. A more didactic personality could have taken it all further. Perhaps I will too when the time is right. Initially all I wanted to do was to document the biography of a soul scaling the heights of freedom...I have gone my own way, as best I could; then, looking back, I did my best to describe the path I had taken."[7]

Many people have written about *The Philosophy of Freedom*, tracing the various threads of thought that unfold across the 14 chapters, analyzing its influence on Steiner's later work, showing its significance for various aspects of

---

edition and the revised edition. The first edition is full of a radical youthful exuberance; Steiner's commitment to individualism comes through much more strongly. The second edition is tamer, more refined.

7   Rudolf Steiner, *Briefe Band II*, p. 232

cultural life. This is not the place to try and replicate or summarize the extant body of literature. In the present context, what interests me is the relation of the path Steiner describes here, "the path [he] had taken," to his later work on meditation.

In the foreword to the 1918 edition, Steiner calls attention to this relationship:

> If anyone should be astonished at not finding in this book any reference to that region of the world of spiritual experience described in my later writings, I would ask him to bear in mind that it was not my purpose at that time to set down the results of spiritual research, but first to *lay the foundations on which such results could rest.*[8] (Italics by McA)

The *Philosophy of Freedom* marks the last stage in Steiner's decade long struggle to articulate the philosophical and epistemological basis for his experience of the spiritual. In it, he addresses two questions: the possibility of individual freedom and the source of individual moral action. At the center of the discussion of both of these questions lies the experience of the nature of intuitive thinking or, as Steiner also formulated it, the intuitive nature of thinking. It is on this experience that everything rests. In an addition to the last chapter written in 1918, Steiner writes about the second part of the book:

> This presents intuitive thinking as man's inwardly experienced spiritual activity. To understand the

---

8   Rudolf Steiner, *The Philosophy of Freedom,* p. xxv

nature of thinking by experiencing it amounts to
a knowledge of the freedom of intuitive thinking.[9]

Why is this important? The experience of the spiritual
nature of intuitive thinking opens the door to the recognition of thinking's capacity to grasp not only the non-
perceptible reality of objects and events belonging to the
sense world, but also of presences that have only a non-
sense-perceptible reality, the "objects" and "events" of the
spiritual world. Thinking is not only not dependent on the
sense-world: for the sense-world, as it were, to make sense,
we depend on thinking. Thinking is, however, not something that simply happens in me like the exchange of gases
across the alveolar membrane. It only happens if I do it.
Thinking is, in fact, a will activity.

Yet, if I immerse myself in the activity of thinking, I
find myself moving in a world of contextual lawfulness, in
which concepts and ideas express their relationships with
one another as well as to the world that opens itself to
my senses. I can have the experience that although thinking only happens when I will it, what happens in thinking
belongs to something beyond me, something to which I too
belong. Here the will-activity of thinking changes and takes
on a gently receptive, participatory quality. In experiencing
the activity of thinking, I discover an aspect of myself that is
intimately connected to the world of ideas and insights that
gives meaning to and illuminates the world I encounter
through the senses. I perceive myself as a spiritually active
being; I intuit my own spiritual nature. And in doing so I

9   Ibid., p. 221

discover within myself a space from which I have the possibility of placing myself freely in relationship to the world around me, a space from which I can conceive and engage in actions that bear the spiritual signature of my own self.

In many ways, *The Philosophy of Freedom* is the first step on the meditative path that Rudolf Steiner later describes. The intuitive recognition of the self as spirit is simultaneously the experience of your own spirituality. Not in a general sense, as in: all humans are in essence spiritual beings. No, it is the concrete experience: you experience your own spirituality. It is somewhat similar to walking into an oak pillar in a dark room. There is no question in your mind that it is there. It is both exhilarating and humbling. And it leaves you feeling excruciatingly lonely, quite simply because it is an experience that is very difficult to articulate. It is one of those experiences that change everything.

> Once experienced, the world of spiritual perception cannot appear to man as something foreign to him, because in his intuitive thinking he already has an experience which is purely spiritual in character. Such a world of spiritual perception is discussed in a number of writings which I have published since this book first appeared. *The Philosophy of Freedom* forms the philosophical foundation for these later writings. For it tries to show that the experience of thinking, when rightly understood, is in fact an experience of the spirit.[10]

In this work, in which Rudolf Steiner describes an

---

10   Ibid.

epistemological space within which his spiritual perceptions ring true, he also does something that most philosophers have a tendency to steer clear of: he describes his experience of thinking from within, rather than analyzing it from outside. You might say that he approaches thinking as Goethe did plants. He lets thinking speak and listens to what it has to say about itself. In doing so, he becomes cognizant not only of qualitative aspects of the living world of ideas, but also of aspects of the self in its relation both to the body and to the spirit. And, as with every good Goethean observation, each recognition birthed a wealth of new questions.

The experienced conceptualization of the self as an active spiritual presence in human consciousness has consequences for our understanding of human nature. An anthropological approach in which this plays no role will search for other explanations of human individuality. A scientific understanding that only acknowledges the reality of matter will explain it in terms of bodily functions; a transcendent approach will turn elsewhere for answers. The discovery, however, of the self as an active factor in the unfolding of human consciousness leads to questions concerning the nature of the self and its relation to the body. The struggle to cast light on this question will remain a central theme in Rudolf Steiner's life until his death in 1925. Much of what he develops as meditative practice focuses on various aspects of this relationship.

III.   Inner Life

I too with my soul and body,

We, a curious trio, picking, wandering on our way...

Walt Whitman

Rudolf Steiner's work and the path of intentional growth that arose out of it revolves around the inner life of the soul. Unlike many of his contemporaries, he did not ascribe to the rise of a psychological approach that, by the end of the 19th century had "more or less abandoned the soul and replaced it with the mind."[11] He had learned to know the soul as a space within which the self grappled with the realities of its existence. He experienced the soul and its modalities as primary rather than secondary phenomena.

The soul is a riddle. It is one of the grand riddles, one of those riddles that gives meaning to life. For Steiner, the soul was as much a region to explore as Antarctica was for Ernest Shackleton. Like Freud and Adler, Steiner turned his gaze inwards. But unlike them, his interest was focused primarily on the positive forces of the soul, the forces that

---

11   Edward S. Reed, *From Soul to Mind*, p. 3

allow the soul to become evermore the expression of the spiritual presence he had experienced in his observations of thinking. He was less interested in what the soul had become than in the path of the soul becoming, and quite specifically, the path of the soul becoming the expression of its self. Early on, he recognized that if the soul were to become the expression of the spiritual or higher self, one would need to intentionally create within the soul the conditions that would support this process of inner development. This is something that can only be done from within. The self must become the agent of its own evolution. The soul is the stage upon which this evolution occurs.

The soul lives, Steiner would say in 1904, between the body and the spirit, with emphasis on the word *lives*. The soul is a space of activity, of movement, an inner space where past and future meet to shape the experienced present. We experience this inner movement in three ways: as thinking, as feeling, and as the mystery of the will. The movement of the soul comes to expression in its purest form in what we experience as feeling; it finds itself reflected in the mental images that initially form the basis of thinking; and it flows out into the world in action, in willing. These three aspects of the soul live and mediate between the bodily reality of human existence and the spiritual reality of human becoming. The soul itself is neither body nor spirit, but is affected by both what comes to it from the body and by what comes to it from the spirit. It is an inner space of consciousness and non-consciousness, of connectedness and separation, of knowing and giving; it is a space of sublime alchemy, where

world and self meet and permeate one another, a space
of encounter, where both the encountered and she-who-
encounters are transformed. It is the space where the self
becomes aware of itself. This too is an encounter. The soul
is a space both of repose and of turmoil, a space, that can
grow narrow and cold with fear or warm and wide when
filled with trust; it can recoil in disgust or flow out beyond
itself in wonder. There are things that linger in the soul:
memories, impressions, and encounters. The ever-moving
soul flows around these; they give its movements direction,
like the pattern of waves in the water flowing over the
pebbles in a stream. Change the configuration of the stones,
the pattern of the flow changes also.

Though it lives in the middle, the soul is not merely a
function of the polar unity we can describe as body and
spirit. The soul has its own configuration. This configuration affects the way it mediates between body and spirit.
Yes, the stones change the flow of the water, but the flow
will also be different depending on the nature of the water.
The sluggish blighted water trapped in a canal bears within
it different possibilities of movement than the cold, clear,
lively waters of an alpine spring.

Steiner describes a path of meditation and soul practice
that serves both to reconfigure the stones and to transform
the nature of the water flowing over them.

The English word "soul" can be traced back to the Proto-
Germanic word *saiwala*, which is believed to have denoted
"coming from or belonging to the sea." But whereas water
can be held at least momentarily in your hands, the soul

cannot. It has no weight, no size. It is immaterial. Its immateriality is pure movement. Not just any movement, but one that is always in relation to other movements. You could perhaps think of a dance, a dance that never stops: a dance of fluid receptivity. When the soul becomes stiff, when it ceases to move with and in the world, when no encounters cause it to question or to wonder, when it can no longer be moved by what comes to meet it, the soul in some way ceases to be soul. In this way, too, the soul has an innate similarity with water. Water also dies to some extent when it is no longer free to move, when trapped by something with which it can no longer enter into a relationship.

No image or metaphor for the soul would be complete if it did not include the qualities of light and color. These, too, move, but their motion is different from that of water. Water moves around obstacles, shaping them and, in turn, being shaped by them. Light and color appear as qualities of illumination in the soul. Light calls forth form and color from the darkness. Venture out in the early hours of the morning on a clear, moonless night. Find a place away from the lights of a house, a town or a city. Enjoy the darkness, the starlit dome of the heavens, and wait for the dawning of a new day. It is important to begin in the darkness, before the stars have begun to pale with the coming of the dawn. You must experience the world in darkness to fully grasp the meaning of the light. Without the light, the world is shapeless and colorless.

As the night gives way to the slow and gentle coming of the day, it first acquires shape, delineated by varied shades of gray and then, as the light grows stronger, color. These appear shyly at first, their voices muted, gentle. But as the light grows, the world comes alive with color, a choir of color. The distinctive shapes, which stood out so prominently in the half-light, recede as the colors come to the fore.

The soul, of course, knows its own darkness, a darkness that yearns for the light. In Steiner's experience, the initial source of light in the soul was thinking. And color? In his *Meditations*, Marcus Aurelius, the contemplative emperor of the Roman Empire, wrote: "The soul becomes dyed with the color of its thoughts." You might ask yourself: "What are the thoughts that color my soul?"

Pondering this, one discovers that the content of thoughts are only one part of the picture. How I think these thoughts affects the quality with which they light up in my soul and infuse it with color. A good thought, thought well, radiates through my whole being. The same thought can have a very different effect: its presence in the soul can be dull and muddying. This is especially a problem of our time, with its propensity for unassailable sound-bites. The truth of a thought is never divorced from its expression. The colors of a true thought expressed without conviction or understanding are dull and muddied or metallic and hard.

The path Steiner describes focuses on the intentional transformation of this flowing inner reality with its obstacles, flow patterns, light, and color: the inner life of the soul. The tool that the soul has most readily at hand to intentionally effect this transformation is thinking: not having thoughts, but forming thoughts, experiencing them in meditation and living with them.

It is unusual today to think of thinking as the key to unlocking the spiritual dimensions of the soul. Thinking is not something most of us associate with spiritual experience. In fact, spiritual experience seems to be closest when we are not thinking, when we drop the defenses of thinking and simply let ourselves be. Overcoming or quieting thinking as a first step towards spiritual communion is an essential aspect of many popular meditative practices. And there is no question that there is a side of thinking that must come to rest if you are to focus yourself on anything at all. Shunryu Suzuki in his gem of a book *Zen Mind, Beginner's Mind* called it the "small mind."

> If your mind is related to something outside itself, that mind is a small mind, a limited mind.[12]

You must let this come to rest if you are to experience the quality of mindfulness and activity that it both points toward and hides.

Toward the end of his life, in a series of lectures in which he rearticulated the anthroposophical path, Steiner spoke of this quieting in the following manner:

> In my ordinary thinking I am quite passive. I allow something to happen to me; I let Nature fill me with thoughts. But I will no longer let myself be filled with thoughts. I will place in my consciousness the thoughts I want to have and I will only pass from

---

12   Shunryu Suzuki, *Zen Mind, Beginner's Mind*, p. 35

one thought to another thought through the inner
strength of thinking itself.[13]

In other words, I will consciously take hold of the flow
of thinking, guiding it as it finds its way from one thought
to the next. As I become more capable and thus free in
guiding the soul in thinking, my soul grows peaceful. An
inner stillness arises. What is it that you find in the inner
stillness of the gently quieted and directed soul? The self,
which, turning inward and giving itself direction, allows
itself to come to a state of tensile or attentive receptivity.
The challenge, from Steiner's point of view, is not to deepen
thinking, but rather to strengthen the power of thinking.
Meditation is the practice through which we can do this.

What are the qualities in the moving, living soul that
allow this inward turning and the intentional anticipatory
opening that accompanies it to find something more than
emptiness within?

---

13   Rudolf Steiner, *Anthroposophy, An Introduction*, pp. 30–31

IV.   The Sense World

A lake is the landscape's most beautiful and expressive
feature. It is the earth's eye; looking into which the beholder
measures the depth of his own nature.

Henry David Thoreau

Between writing *The Philosophy of Freedom* and beginning to address the question posed above, something happened in Rudolf Steiner's life that, according to him, changed both his experience of the inner life of the soul and of the individual's relationship to the spirit. It occurred toward the end of his tenure at the Goethe-Schiller Archive in Weimar, shortly before he moved to Berlin. He writes about it in his autobiography:

> I was 36 years old at the end of my time in Weimar.
> About a year earlier a profound transformation
> began in my soul.

A few lines later, the consequence of this inner shift:

> A new attentiveness for sense-perceptible phenomena awakened within me.[14]

---

14   Rudolf Steiner, *Autobiography*, p. 163

At 35, Rudolf Steiner became aware, in a new way, of the sense world. The thinker, fully at home in the experienced reality of ideas, awakens to something that had to that moment made little impression on him: the world that reveals itself through the senses.

Although his autobiography bears eloquent witness to "the clear, unbroken line" of his own development, the above passage speaks of the non-linearity of that line.[15] The discovery of the sense world came as something of a surprise. It was an unexpected gift.

It changed everything; but in the way that things change within the context of themselves. An oak in blossom is still an oak, but it is not the late summer oak rich in acorns. Steiner remained Steiner, but he became a different Steiner than he was before. What he was before was no longer there as it had been. Something was new.

What was this new experience?

On a shelf in one corner of my study stands the skull and horns of an impala. I brought it back from Kenya some years ago. I was on a short safari following a conference on Waldorf education in Nairobi, observing the animal life of the Great Rift Valley from the back of an open Land Rover. We were driving through open grassland. The grass was short. There were scattered groups of acacia trees. The only animals in sight were giraffes. They were quite far away. The impala skull lay beneath a group of small trees a short distance from the dirt track. I asked the driver to stop. He smiled and said it wasn't allowed. I told him I wanted the

---

15   Christopher Bamford, in Rudolf Steiner, *Autobiography*, p. vii.

impala horns. He shrugged and brought the Land Rover to a halt. I stepped out of the open door and into Africa.

I remember the moment vividly. I stood there beside the truck for a moment, then set out through the bush, walking briskly but not hurrying, not wanting to attract the attention of any unseen animals. All my senses were alert and open to the world around me. Time ceased to have any meaning. I crossed the open expanse, picked up the skull and returned to the Land Rover. Nothing happened, yet everything had changed. Before leaving the truck, I had seen the African landscape, I had observed the animals. When I stepped out onto the African plain, I was, for a brief moment, *in* Africa. Immersed in the sounds, the smells, the light, the forms of the plants; feeling the uneven ground beneath my feet; acutely aware of my own movement, I felt myself become a part of the landscape. Africa became richer, more majestic, more mysterious; it wrapped itself around me and, in its wholeness, became real.

The French philosopher Maurice Merleau-Ponty wrote about this quality of experience:

> The relations of the sentient to sensible are comparable with those of a sleeper to his slumber: sleep comes when a certain voluntary attitude suddenly receives from outside the confirmation for which it was waiting. I am breathing deeply and slowly in order to summon sleep, and suddenly it is as if my mouth were connected to some great lung outside myself, which alternately calls forth and forces back my breath. A certain rhythm of respiration, which a

moment ago I voluntarily maintained, now becomes my very being, and sleep, until now aimed at as a significance, suddenly becomes a situation. In the same way I give ear, or look in the expectation of a sensation, and suddenly the sensible takes possession of my ear or gaze, and I surrender a part of my body, even my whole body, to this particular manner of vibrating and filling space known as blue or red. Just as a sacrament not only symbolizes, in sensible species, an occupation of Grace, but is also the real presence of God, [...] sensation is literally a form of communion. [...] As I contemplate the blue of the sky I am not set over against it as an acosmic subject; I do not possess it in thought, or spread out towards it some idea of blue such as might reveal the secret of it, I abandon myself to it and plunge into this mystery, it "thinks itself within me." I am the sky itself as it is drawn together and unified, and as it begins to exist for itself; my consciousness is saturated with limitless blue.[16]

In his work on perception, Merleau-Ponty differentiates between "intellectual consciousness" and "sensible consciousness," between the consciousness that allows us to know ourselves knowing about a world we experience as an object outside of ourselves and the quality of consciousness that arises when we immerse ourselves in the living, vital reality through which that world reveals itself to us through our senses. Of the latter he says:

---

16   Maurice Merleau-Ponty, *Phenomenology of Perception*, p. 249

Each time I experience a sensation, I feel that it concerns not my own being, the one for which I am responsible and for which I make decisions, but another self which has already sided with the world, which is already open to certain of its aspects and synchronized with them.[17]

What does Steiner write of his own experience?

I had the feeling that the sense world could show something that only it can reveal…When the sensory realm is approached objectively, free of all subjectivity, it reveals something about which a spiritual philosophy has nothing to say.[18]

With this experience, Steiner's own practice changes. Instead of striving to enter into a spiritual relationship with the world cognitively, exclusively through the medium of thinking, he begins to focus his attention on observation, on letting the sense world reveal to him what only it can reveal. He lives into the world as it offers itself to him: as sensory experience. Until now he had striven to free his thinking from the sense world, to practice and explore the nuances of *sense-free thinking*. Now he shifts that striving. He turns his gaze outward. He senses without thinking. He practices *thought-free sensing*. Through this shift in focus, this shift in practice, he discovers "a new world."

The awakened sensibility for the sense world led Steiner to an enhanced awareness of the two poles of the soul's

17   Ibid., p. 251
18   Rudolf Steiner, *Autobiography*, p. 163

experience. In living into the reality of sensing, he found that "one completely leaves oneself." You enter into a non-conscious, participatory encounter with the sense world: you surrender yourself to an experience of what lives there. In this encounter, you are at one with what lives in that world. Experiencing this world through intentional sensing is different than it is to know about it through thinking. Fourteen years later, in a lecture in Hanover, Steiner spoke about a four-step path to overcoming the limitations of what we normally term "thinking." He described how one can progress through wonder and reverence to a feeling of harmony with the cosmos until one finally achieves the capacity to surrender to the experience of sensing:

> And now we must go on to consider the fruits of this surrender. What do we attain when we have gone forward with our thinking from wonder to reverence, thence to feeling oneself in wisdom-filled harmony with reality and finally to the attitude of surrender—what do we attain? We come at last to this. As we go about the world and observe the plants in all their greenness and admire the changing colors of their blossoms, or as we contemplate the sky in its blueness and the stars with their golden brilliance—not forming judgments but letting the things themselves reveal to us what they are—then if we have really succeeded in learning this "surrender," all things in the world of sense become changed for us, and something is revealed to us in the world of the senses, for which we can find no other word than a

word taken from our own soul life…One who has attained in any high degree to surrender discovers everywhere in the world of the senses *creative will*.[19]

At about the same time, in the first series of lectures outlining what Rudolf Steiner termed "anthroposophy," he spoke of it as a path to the spirit through the senses.

Immersing yourself completely in the qualitative realities of the world we know through the senses, without holding anything back, leads to a new experience of that world. It reveals itself as creative will. What is will? It is an unceasing bubbling forth of creativity and formation. The other pole of the soul's experience comes to expression in the relationship to the world we gain through thinking, Merleau-Ponty's "intellectual consciousness." Immersed, however, in the inner unfolding and blossoming of ideas, Steiner also experienced a quality of will in which he came to recognize the spiritual nature of his own beingness. In the *activity* of thinking, he discovers self-willing; surrendering himself to the *activity* of sensing, he discovers world-willing.

One can live into this rhythm of the spiritual experience of the self in thinking and of the world in sensing. The thinking self can place itself in an intentional relationship to what it encounters in the world; the sensing self is taken up into a world of creative, generative presence. Between the two, life unfolds. For Steiner, the two experiences were contradictory. He didn't feel, though, that there was any need to resolve the contradiction philosophically. In fact, he

---

19 Rudolf Steiner, Lecture in Hanover, December 28, 1911. See *The World of the Senses and the World of the Spirit* (CW 134), p. 21 ff.

felt that to stand fully in the experience of this contradiction was to "have an understanding of life." Wherever the contradiction is experienced as resolved, the world is lifeless, dead. Where there is life, the unresolved contradiction is at work. Life itself is a process of continuously overcoming and recreating contradictions.[20]

It is in the context of this recognition that Steiner gives us what is biographically his first meditation. He writes:

Out of all this, arose in my feeling life an intense desire to devote myself not to a cognitive, theoretical apprehension of the world's riddles, but rather to experiencing them. In order to place myself meditatively in a correct relationship to the world, I repeatedly placed this thought before my soul: "The world is full of riddles. I can approach them cognitively, but that only leads to thought content as a solution to a riddle. But, as I had to tell myself, these riddles do not resolve themselves through thought. Thoughts may bring the soul to a path of resolution; but they do not embody the resolution. In the real world, a riddle comes into being; it appears there; the resolution too comes into being in the real world. A being or process appears through which the resolution is made manifest."[21]

As with Steiner's exploration of thinking, what he is speaking of here has an eminently experiential quality.

---

20   Rudolf Steiner, *Autobiography*, p. 164
21   Ibid.

Either one has had this experience or one hasn't. Thinking about this experience without having had it can be deeply unsatisfying. It leads one away from oneself. On the other hand, the experience of the world as a living riddle to be resolved through action, cognitive or otherwise, opens one to a new dimension of one's self. The self discovered in intuitive thinking is the self that, slowly shedding the outer crutches of necessity, cultural habituation and abiding principles, comes to know itself standing freely and creatively in the world. We can call this "the centering self." It is the self that resolves to submit to the demands of a spiritual practice. It is the self that grows lazy and has to remind itself what it has chosen. It is the self that lets itself be distracted by the smell of coffee wafting down from the kitchen, by the thought of coffee, by the cries of a small child angered by her older siblings, by the buzzing of the mosquitoes in the warmth of a summer evening. It is the self that has to work to create a space for itself within the soul. It is the self that is conscious of itself and of the world around it.

The sensing self is not. It has a non-conscious relation to the world. And even this falls short of grasping the nature of what lives between it and the world. The term relation infers things separate or distinct from one another. The sensing self is neither. It is in and of the world. Even the word "it" doesn't belong to it. It has no it-ness, only is-ness.

The self we first come to know in thinking is the centered self; the self that becomes an experienced reality in sensing is the peripheral self. The spiritual challenge we face today is to bring these two selves into the right relationship with one another, to allow them to illuminate and enliven one another, without denying or trying to negate the dynamic tension that exists between these two realms of experience.

Rudolf Steiner stepped into this space of tension, metaphorically, of course. It is not a space in the spatial sense of the word. You can't step into it. But he stepped into it and practiced holding the two realms of experience free of one another, going fully into one, then going fully into the other: thought-free sensing, then sense-free thinking. What he experienced in one, enhanced his experience of the other, and vice-versa. There was reciprocity between the two experiences. He found his thinking being focused by what came to life in him through his observations, while his experience of the sense world was enriched through the qualities of soul life awakened in him through thinking. He spoke about it in his autobiography as achieving a thinking that conformed to and was deeply rooted in reality. In addition, the meditative integration of these two polar experiences had a deep effect on his feeling life, the pure movement of the soul in the soul.

V.   The Self in the Soul

To find oneself, not in egotistic inner life, but selfless in the world, is true self-knowledge.

Rudolf Steiner

At this point a second facet of the inner path described by Steiner becomes apparent. The conscious guiding of the process of thinking is where the path begins. We can speak of a practice of concentration. In the process of mastering this practice, one begins to make discoveries about the nature of the thinking self and the world of ideas. One learns to trust the activity of thinking. But there is a danger inherent in it. One can become so at home in the world of ideas that one loses one's experienced connection with the sense world, the world that brings one down to earth. And it is, of course, on the earth that we have chosen to be. The practice of thought-free sensing is, if anything, more difficult to master than that of sense-free thinking. In the latter, the thoughts are there to guide you; to practice the former, you have to let go. This letting go is not as easy as it sounds.

The Western mind tends to have a somewhat adversarial relation to the things around it. Perhaps adversarial is too strong a word. Confrontational? Oppositional? It sets us apart. It tells us that the tree is there, and we are here. In the very first stirrings of the conscious *it is*, is also the *I am,* as well as the *I am not it.* I am I, and it is it. The tree is the tree; it is not me, I am not it. I can walk up to the tree, put my arms around it, feel the roughness of its bark against my skin. I can leap up, grasp hold of one of its branches and swing myself up into the tree. I am in it, but still not of it. The relationship of the Western mind to the world is rooted in this quality of encounter. I bump up against the world, and the world becomes in me a mental image.

This experience has led to a wealth of philosophical literature. Why? Because inherent in the experience is a problem. A problem that is not that easy to solve as long as one continues to think about it with the limitations of a mind that only knows of itself when it bumps into something. I can know that I have a mental image of something out there, but what I don't seem to be able to know is whether or not that of which I have formed a mental image corresponds in fact with the mental image I have formed. This is a logical consequence of the spectator theory of human consciousness.

Once I remove human consciousness from any direct and unmediated relation to the world in which it awakens, I open the possibility that what consciousness reveals to me has but a tenuous connection to whatever has stimulated it. The question: Does the picture I form of the world around me within the reaches of my consciousness have any true or immediate connection with that of which it is forming a picture? is certainly one of the great existential questions of our time.

In 1994, the African shaman Malidoma Patrice Somé published a memoir of his path back to his traditional roots and beliefs. This document sheds light on certain aspects of the challenge that lies at the root of Western consciousness. Malidoma was born and spent his earliest years in an African tribal setting more or less untouched by Western thought. His was a world of elemental magic and ritual completely embedded in an experienced cosmology of ancestral beings and nature spirits. This changed when, at the age of four, he was removed from the village by Jesuit missionaries and taken away to be educated in their schools. His childhood and youth were spent far from his home, within the rigid discipline of the mission schools, where he was forbidden to take solace in any aspects of the life he had known as a young child, including his mother tongue.

For the next 16 years, Malidoma's life was completely defined by the rhythms and demands of the mission school, and then later, the seminary. He became known as Patrice, and, step by step, he was initiated into the mysteries of Western thought. This process was so successful that by the time Malidoma reached his late teens, he was seriously thinking of going on to become a priest of the Catholic Church. However, try as they might, the priests could not completely quash the youth's sense of dignity and justice. These led him repeatedly into conflict with the embodied pettiness of some his more dictatorial teachers. One such instance brought his time in the seminary to a close. He had just finished writing a French dictation and was going back over his text to check for mistakes. The teacher approached his desk, read the text over his shoulder, and then pointed to two words toward the end of the text. They had been misspelled. When Malidoma made a move to correct them, the priest knocked his hand aside. Malidoma tried again. Once more the priest knocked his hand: He had found the mistakes not Malidoma. The argument escalated, both men losing their tempers. Finally, the priest struck Malidoma across the face. In a moment, Malidoma was on his feet, unwilling any longer to submit to the priest's punishments. He was a young man now, 20 years old, large and strong. He was ready to stand up for himself. The altercation came to an abrupt end when the priest crashed through the window and plummeted to the earth below. Only then did Malidoma stop to consider the consequences of what he had done.

Minutes later he plunged into the jungle at the edge of the seminary compound and, for the first time in 16 years, was back in Africa.

Malidoma returned to his native village. His sister found him, a stranger, sitting beside the mudded gateway when she returned from working in the fields. Only his mother recognized him. Yet after all these years they were unable to speak with one another; they no longer shared a common language. Only his sister, who had spent a year at the Mission School, could speak a little French.

His presence upset the placid life of the village. Although he is one of theirs, he no longer belongs to them. He thinks like a white man, not like a Dagara. His knowledge is worthless within the context of their lives. Of the things that do have value within this context, he knows nothing. Even worse, not only does he know nothing, the way he knows things creates an unsurpassable barrier for learning. The elders spend hours pondering his situation in council. Finally, they come to a decision. The only way for him to find his place among them again is through the ritual of initiation to which every young Dagara male must submit himself.

Every true path of initiation is a path wrought with danger. No one ventures on such a path knowing ahead of time what the outcome will be. No one who steadfastly weathers the trials comes out unchanged. In Malidoma's case, the elders were uncertain whether he had the inner sense of unity to survive the trials at all. There was every indication that submitting to the initiation, crippled as he was by the ways of thinking acquired from the white men, would cost him his life.

When the time for the ritual arrived, Malidoma found himself trekking naked into the bush with a group of about sixty 13-to 14-year-old boys. He was 21. The rituals would extend over a period of six weeks, during which time the boys would remain secluded, accompanied by a "coach" and five elders. The first trial began on the morning of the boys' second day in the bush. They were told to go off, find a tree, and look at it until they saw something.

> The tree I chose was about ten meters high, with a trunk less than a meter in diameter: a yila tree. I

chose a comfortable place to sit and began staring. The sun had risen higher and the freezing temperature of the morning was quickly turning warm. I gazed at the tree faithfully, as I had been told to. For the next five hours nothing happened. The exercise became more and more exasperating, since I had nothing but a tree to look at.[22]

Malidoma gazed at the tree with eyes trained by the missionaries, and what did he see? A tree. As the day went on, boys began to wander back to camp as they completed the task. By the end of the day, only Malidoma still sat looking at his tree. The others had done what they had set out to do: They had seen something. Only Malidoma was unable to see anything but a tree. Alone he made his way into the bush encampment in the dark; alone he returned the next day to gaze again at his tree.

This question of seeing beyond what something appears to be begins to truly matter when I start to struggle to understand something or someone; when I am no longer satisfied with knowing *about* things and people, and begin to want to truly know and understand them, in Steiner's words, when they become riddles for me. Then I am faced with the void, the expanse, the barrier that exists between what takes place within my mind, and that which occurs around me. I throw my arms around the tree. Not only is it not me, I find that I have no immediate sense of certainty concerning its beingness.

---

22   Malidoma Patrice Somé, *Of Water and the Spirit*, pp. 203-219

This lack of certainty arises in the soul when I begin to think about *how* I know. If I don't reflect on my own knowing, the world is what it appears to be, and I can respond or react to it as I have become accustomed to. I explain its riddles within the framework of the theoretical context in which I have been trained. If I come from a religious background, I see the world in terms of faith; if my background is colored by agnosticism and materialistic science, I will view the world in terms of the premises inherent to these ways of thinking. Both have one thing in common: they are based on the belief that the world is "out there" and I am "in here" and what is "out there" is separated from what is "in here" by an unbridgeable chasm. This chasm lies "behind" what is commonly called the percept, the conceptually integrated array of sense impressions, which reflects itself within my consciousness as a mental image. The percept is how the self-conscious soul holds the sense world at bay. When the world is reduced to a percept, it ceases to be a presence. Within my soul, the percept can be raised to the world of ideas; it can become a conceptual presence in my life. The path of the transformation of my relationship to the percept and the implication of this transformation for individual action are what Rudolf Steiner describes in *The Philosophy of Freedom.* There he develops a spiritual philosophy as the basis for a relation to the world that he termed ethical individualism.

With the discovery of the sense world, Rudolf Steiner becomes aware of a new dimension of reality. He enters into the presence of what lies behind the veil of the percept. He awakens in what Merleau-Ponty termed "sensible consciousness" and is able to know the experience of the divine: the creative will.

It is helpful to think deeply about the difference between these two poles of soul experience. Simple situations make this difference quite clear. Take for example skiing. You can sit at home in your favorite chair in the middle of summer and think about skiing. You can remember slopes that you have skied, call to mind extraordinary times you might have had on the slopes, you can live into your recollections letting them carry you off into your imagination. This act of imagination can grow so intense that you actually feel the bite of the wind against your cheeks, that you can taste the freshness of the air. You can immerse yourself in this imaginative experience and discover aspects of skiing or of yourself that only light up in your consciousness because you now give them the opportunity. Many things are possible, you may even discover previously unknown aspects of the sport. But some things are not possible. You can never break your leg. You will never find yourself sitting with an intriguing stranger in the chairlift. Such encounters are only possible if you go skiing.

I had a friend who decided one fall to learn how to sail. He took it very seriously. He bought books, learned all the terminology, even took a course on navigation at the local yacht club. When the spring came, I invited him to go for a sail with me. He came down to the dock, excited and looking forward to putting all his studies to the test. I had brought the boat in from its mooring and laid it alongside.

He swung himself down quite jauntily, let go of the rail and I watched his face turn white as a ghost. He grasped desperately for a line, something to hold onto, and said, "Oh, it moves!" Only by stepping off the solidity of the dock could he experience the movement of a floating boat beneath his feet. This is a realm of experience we do not normally encounter in thinking, but which is implicit in everything we do in the sense world, even if we are not always aware of it. Things happen in the sense world in a way they do not in the world of ideas. At least initially.

Within the sense world, we are constantly present in a world of will. It is within the world of will that the human biography unfolds. It is here that we make those encounters that shape our lives for better or for worse; this is the world where life takes place. Take a moment and think back over the course of your own life. How much of what you have become, how many of your accomplishments, do you owe to yourself and your own devices, and how much do you owe to what others have given you?

We are often inclined to take credit for our accomplishments and blame others for our failures. Try turning that around. Look out into the world and ask what it has given you that made it possible for you to achieve what you have been able to achieve. I have been a teacher for many years. Looking back, I have to say that whatever I have been able to do has been thanks to the children and young people who have been in my classes. They made me into a teacher. I did not do it. There have been times I bungled the opportunity they gave me. In those moments I was trying to be something or some way that was not in accordance with the reality of the situation at hand. That was my fault, not theirs. What I brought to the process of becoming was the willingness to learn.

With some practice we can learn to recognize that what we encounter in the world—the people, the aspects of nature, and the interactions that make an impression on our soul and that live on within us—shape us and give us the opportunity to become ourselves.

Toward the end of his life, Rudolf Steiner wrote about this relationship in the following manner:

> Man's destiny comes to meet him from the world that he knows through his senses. If he can become aware of his own activity in the working of his destiny, his real self rises up before him not only out of his inner being but out of the sense-world too.[23]

What do I find in the world that comes to meet me when I turn my senses outward, looking, listening, sensing? Myself. This is not the conscious, reflective self, the worried self, the strategic self; it is the self of the will, the sculpting self, the shaping self, the karmic self. This self is present among the multitude of activities that lie beyond the veil of the percept. If I am to find my self, I must turn toward the world, I must not think of myself, of my own comfort or desires. These are for the self what the percept is for the sense-world: maya or illusion. Attachment to them traps the self within the narrow limitations

---

23   Rudolf Steiner, *Anthroposophical Leading Thoughts*, p. 39

of its own conception of itself. I become self-centered, and, in doing so, blind to the self at work in the world around me. I lose the connection to the forces of my own unfolding. I am not only cut off from myself, but from the active presence of the spiritual in the surrounding world.[24]

---

24   Today, it seems essential from a spiritual perspective to become aware of this dilemma. Much of what we have grown accustomed to in the fast-paced virtual world of an increasingly digitalized society exacerbates the problem. If we don't become conscious of the sculptural, reciprocal relationship between the forces of the self in the world and the forces of the self in the soul, we can very easily find ourselves trapped in an illusion, struggling to navigate our lives guided by extrinsic markers: wealth, social acceptance, etc., or other people's teachings and values. These replace one's own inner sense of direction and in the long run leave the soul empty, cut off from the source of its inner vitality.

VI.   A Spiritual Discipline

Whether our action is wholesome or unwholesome
depends on whether that action or deed arises from
a disciplined or undisciplined state of mind. It is felt
that a disciplined mind leads to happiness and an
undisciplined mind leads to suffering, and in fact it
is said that bringing about discipline within one's
mind is the essence of the Buddha's teaching.

Dalai Lama

The path of inner transformation that Rudolf Steiner
followed and then described, rests on these two experiences: the experience of the divine nature of the human
will in thinking and the experience of the divine presence
of the cosmic will in sensing. It arises from a deep inner
conviction of the essential unity between the will that
works within the human soul and the creative forces of the
cosmos, and from the recognition that the human being,
the individual human being, has a unique role to play in the
rhythmic unfolding of cosmic evolution. The spiritual path
Steiner described rests on this recognition. It is not a path
of heightened consciousness for the sake of heightened
consciousness; it is not a path of healthy well-being for the

sake of healthy well-being. It is a path of service, a path of intentional action. It begins with a heightened awareness of what lives in the world around us and leads to the capacity to act selflessly in response to what this world asks of us.

It is a path that, when taken, changes one's life.

Rudolf Steiner began to speak publicly about the nature and results of his own spiritual path in Berlin in the autumn of 1900. Two years later, he became the general secretary of the newly formed German branch of the Theosophical Society. In May 1904, he received approval from Annie Besant to take on esoteric students of his own. At this point, he began to speak specifically and concretely about a path of inner development that leads to a conscious experience of the spiritual in the world. Initially, he spoke to a rather intimate circle of people interested in questions of the spirit. A still smaller circle of individuals turned explicitly to Steiner for spiritual guidance. These were individuals who, for one reason or another, committed themselves to a regular spiritual practice under his tutelage. Much of what today is readily available for public consumption concerning the anthroposophical path was initially articulated for this circle. It was, in the Aristotelian sense, esoteric and focused on the development of yet to be uncovered or occult capacities.

It is important to understand what the term "occult" meant to Rudolf Steiner. In relation to the path of schooling, it does not refer to what is often bandied about as occult knowledge. The primary focus of the path is not to enable one to acquire occult or esoteric knowledge.

Rudolf Steiner speaks of this path in relation to a specific aspect of human becoming: "There lie within the human soul seed-like forces or capacities. These can only germinate and grow if the human being chooses to cultivate them." In Steiner's understanding, an occult or inner path of schooling begins with the choice to cultivate these nascent capabilities. This is a choice one makes consciously. It is an intentional choice. One is fully cognizant of the fact that one is embarking on a path that will change the way one relates to the surrounding world. There is a moral, existential quality to the way Rudolf Steiner speaks about this choice. He speaks of dangers and possible harm. One cannot mistake the earnestness in his tone. The path is real. Awakening the seed-like forces of spiritual awareness in the soul leads one to a deeper, more intimate connection with one's world and the forces that shape it.

Occult development is the path from a cognitively safe, self-centered relationship with our surroundings to a willed, world-centered relationship of conscious engagement and participation. It rests upon the mystery of the human will.

As mentioned above, much of what is readily available today concerning this path of will-borne transformation was originally published for a limited circle of spiritually interested individuals. Rudolf Steiner began to work with them on the more intimate questions of soul development. At the outset, both in what he published and in what he shared with those who turned to him for guidance, he described required practices, practices that would bring about conditions within the soul that are conducive to healthy occult development. In contrast to many Eastern practices and other religious practices, these are neither postural nor behavioral requirements. They focus on achieving an attentive intentional relationship to the life of the soul. Steiner's descriptions of the life of the soul focus on its three different qualities of relationship or relatedness, initially to the surrounding world. As mentioned above, these three qualities of relatedness are experienced in the soul as thinking, feeling, and willing.

While modern psychology does differentiate between these three functions, they are viewed as three aspects of how the brain responds to external stimulus. They are viewed as "mental" functions. This view arose initially in the second half of the 19th century and, as the exploration of various neurological functions brought new insight into the functioning of the brain and nervous system, became increasingly popular among both scientists and laymen.[25]

Rudolf Steiner took issue with this approach early on. In his experience, thinking, feeling, and will were not merely variations on a common theme—the response of the brain to external stimuli—they were the inner expression of different qualities of experience. When speaking with the teachers of the first Waldorf school in the late summer of 1919, he spoke about these differences, characterizing the different states of consciousness connected with each of them. Thinking, he said, can be likened to the quality of consciousness we know when we are awake; willing can be likened to the quality of conscious we know when we

---

25 Compare Edward S. Reed, *From Soul to Mind*.

are asleep; and feeling, which lies in between, brings itself
to expression within us as a dream-like state. In thinking
we have a waking consciousness because we experience
the world in the form of a picture. This allows us to differentiate ourselves from the world. Feeling consciousness
and willing consciousness place us, however, in relation not
to the world as picture, but as realness. Both feeling and
willing, the latter more deeply than the former, are woven
into the unseen forces at work in the world around us.
These states of participation or oneness do not, under normal conditions, rise up into the light of consciousness we
know in thinking. They exist under the surface, informing
and guiding us in our relation to the world around without
our being aware of them.

Rudolf Steiner's earliest spiritual exercises, those he
termed fundamental requirements for any occult or will-
borne path of inner development, focused on bringing
these undercurrents of participatory relatedness into the
realm of individual intent, into the realm of the conscious
I. They form the basis of the preparatory stage of a modern
path of initiation. They are exercises to be mastered if one
wishes to follow the path Steiner described.

The original descriptions of these exercises were distributed to the small circle of esoteric students on two
mimeographed sheets. The first contained six exercises, the
second four rules or resolutions. The first six appear also in
Steiner's more public descriptions of the anthroposophical path; the second four only on this privately distributed
mimeographed sheet.

The first six exercises are:

1. Cultivate absolutely clear thinking by practicing attentiveness with a simple object
2. Perform a freely chosen task each day
3. Practice equanimity
4. Practice positivity
5. Practice open-mindedness
6. Practice all five in various combinations

Of these first six exercises, only the first one can be practiced in seclusion, and even it has as its central focus something that belongs to the perceptible world. (Rudolf Steiner is emphatic in this regard. Don't immerse yourself in great thoughts or in your own ideas. Focus your attention on something simple and practical: a straight pin, a pencil, or a paperclip. Learn to let its reality, its connectedness guide your thinking.) All the other exercises must be practiced in the stream of daily life. One must learn to remember in this stream to perform the task one has set for oneself; it is in this stream that one cultivates equanimity, positivity, open-mindedness; it is in this stream that the soul becomes increasingly aware of the strength of its own presence. The reality of one's own life is the sanctuary or temple, within which this esoteric path unfolds. Life itself is the master.

These exercises are for the meditant as finger exercises are for the musician. You begin with them, struggle with them, return to them. They become an integral part of your daily life. They give the soul an inner attunement and create the steady undercurrent upon which meditative consciousness can rest. They serve to give the movement of the soul direction and a sculptural beauty, which radiates through everything you do. You learn to think clearly, become able to differentiate between what is essential and what is non-essential; you are increasingly able to do what you set out to do; you become a steady, open, interested presence in the lives of those surrounding you. Life becomes more interesting, increasingly revelatory, and more demanding. As you master these exercises, you begin also to bring to awareness the inner capacities, the dormant capacities of the soul. Aspects of the soul's relatedness to the surrounding world that previously had gone unnoticed become apparent. The world reveals itself in new ways. You become more aware of your connectedness to all that happens around you.

These changes are, however, intimately connected to the way you approach the exercises and, of course, dependent on the actual practice. Anyone who has approached these exercises with single-minded determination to prove to the world that, yes, I can do Steiner's six basic exercises, soon tends to lose interest in them. Any reasonably disciplined person can do them, although the unassuming nature of the exercises themselves tends to lead one to forget about them. Am I speaking from experience? Yes. I have forgotten some one or another of these exercises many times. Initially, this presented an almost unsurpassable barrier to mastery. On the evening of the fourth or fifth day of an exercise, I would discover, when looking back over my day that I had completely forgotten about it. The novelty of the exercise wears off quite quickly. With the novelty gone, all one is left with is a feeling of faithfulness or loyalty to oneself: it was, after all, I who chose to do this exercise. If I let it fall by the wayside out of laziness, forgetfulness, lassitude or simply because I have gotten so caught up in my day that other things became more important to me, I have been unfaithful to myself. It is myself that I have let down.

Mastering these exercises demands a gentle, steady will. They are exercises to be approached lovingly. Once you have taken the first hurdle of actually doing the exercises on a regular basis, you can begin to discover that each exercise calls forth specific activities in the soul. The concentration exercise, for example, becomes livelier as you learn to be attentive to the object upon which you are focusing your thoughts. This attentiveness takes on a listening quality. Your thinking begins to let itself be guided by the object. Time ceases to play a role. You can lose yourself entirely in the object of your attention. There are similar soul activities or gestures that accompany each of the exercises:

1. Concentration—Attentiveness
2. Intentional action—Being present
3. Equanimity—Interest
4. Positivity—Gratitude
5. Open-mindedness—Wonder

As these soul activities or gestures expand and grow stronger, you find your relationship to the world changes. Calmness pervades your being. You become less excitable, less inclined to be annoyed, more restrained in your judgments. You find yourself becoming more attentive, more present; the world becomes more interesting, full of things to be thankful for, and a constant source of wonder. You become more receptive and in tune with what is happening around you; the soul becomes permeated with a feeling of trust: for the world, for others, and for yourself. The growing presence of the creative, generative willing self in the soul comes to expression in this trusting embrace of your life. The blossoming of trust marks the "end" of the first stage of the journey.

"End" shall, however, remain in quotation marks. Each end is a new beginning, a spiraling outward as it were. These six basic and essential exercises accompany one for as long as one remains on the inner path. They support the development of individual soul capacities, each of which can grow infinitely. You can always become more attentive, more present, more interested, more grateful, more full of wonder and more trusting. Just as you can always become more human.

When he first gave these exercises to the small circle of individuals who had turned to him explicitly for guidance in their spiritual practice, Rudolf Steiner recommended that they focus specifically on each exercise, in the order he had described them, for a month. The whole cycle would encompass six months. This was the preparatory work for further esoteric training. The final paragraph of this first description of the basic or essential practices closes with the following words:

> [...] the six exercises described overcome the harmful influence other occult exercises can have, so that only their beneficial influences remain. Secondly,

these exercises alone ensure that efforts in meditation and concentration will have a positive result.[26]

The biggest challenge one faces when one begins to tread the path of the seeker—any path of inner development—is the heightened awareness of one's own self. If not accompanied by an intentional opening of the soul to the healing, guiding, and corrective forces of the surrounding world, this heightened self-awareness can easily turn in upon itself and lead to an unproductive self-centeredness, a skewed sense of one's significance in and for the world. The initial six exercises balance this innate tendency of all modern spiritual schooling. They do this by leading you out into the world; it becomes your teacher. It is in relationship with the world that your newfound awareness is tested and made whole.

These first six exercises were followed by four rules of conduct that allow you to constantly observe to what extent the fundamental gestures of soul activity have taken hold in your life. In his introduction, Steiner returns again to the problem of heightened self-awareness and says:

> All esoteric training, particularly when it progresses to higher stages, can lead the pupil only into harm and confusion if such rules are not observed. But as long as one strives to live in accordance with them there is no cause to fear embarking on such a training.[27]

---

26 Rudolf Steiner, *Guidance in Esoteric Training*, p. 24
27 Ibid., p. 25

It doesn't matter if one isn't satisfied with one's own ability to follow them. This should not lead to discouragement.

> It will suffice if one honestly strives, in every area of life, to remember these rules. Such honesty must, above all, be honesty towards oneself. Many deceive themselves in this respect, believing their striving to be a true one. Yet if they would examine themselves more closely they would find a good deal of concealed egoism and refined feelings of self-worth lurking in the background.[28]

Steiner goes on to say that the four rules of conduct that follow help one overcome these lurking feelings, this inner lack of honesty toward oneself about one's intentions, one's hopes and fears, that is constantly creating unseen barriers and illusions of progress upon the path. For anyone intending to follow this path toward an increasingly spiritually rich experience of the world, an honest acceptance of one's own self is imperative. You cannot change those things of which you are not willing to become aware. If you are not willing to look upon yourself with the same equanimity and clarity you strive to bring to bear upon the world, you will remain unable to chart the course of your own transformation. Like a ship without a rudder, you will be at the mercy of the winds and waves, drifting without a compass upon an uncharted ocean.

The first six exercises allow you to achieve a growing intentional presence in your soul's response to the world;

---

28 Ibid.

the following four lead you inward: the practice of them enables you to both become the sculptor of the soul's inner configuration and develop a quality of steadfastness. You begin, as it were, to consciously bring color to the soul, weaving your own patterns and gestures into the tapestry illuminating your consciousness.

1.) I will allow no unexamined ideas to become part of my conceptual reality.

One of the results of the development of Western thought is that we normally encounter the world through the filter of the concepts and mental images we have acquired. As Goethe once pointed out, we tend to see only what we already know. We assimilate or adopt much of our knowledge without ever reflecting on its validity. It is merely an accumulation of the views common to our surroundings and, unexamined, becomes the basis for many of our inclinations, judgments, and prejudices. As such, it stands between the world and us. Because it has been adopted unexamined, it does not have an immediate, intimate relatedness to the forces of the emergent self. It is, to some extent, a foreign object and serves to color my relationship with the world in ways I am unaware of and in a manner in which I am not completely present. On the other hand, it gives my behavior conventional predictability that allows me to function within my social surroundings. In many ways, I fit into and am carried by my surroundings because of these unquestioned, shared notions.

The challenge to examine before adopting ideas does not mean discarding everything I have already acquired. It first means stepping back and exploring the ideas and imagery that I rarely turn my attention toward. It means questioning my usually unquestioned assumptions. These may be as mundane as "Every kitchen needs a dishwasher," or "Vinyl siding is better than wood"; they may reflect social conditioning such as "All children should go to school," or "Good people go to heaven when they die"; they may be facets of a specific world view, "Humans are basically no different than animals." I was raised in an intensely scientific environment: my father was a professor of marine biology, my mother a chemist. The idea that Darwinian theory could be questioned came initially as a major shock to me. Yet only by working through Darwin's thought did I begin to understand how he came to the ideas he had and also begin to see to what extent they could only reflect a partial understanding of the phenomena of change and evolution.

Questioning your deeply held assumptions can be extremely uncomfortable, yet if you take it up, you begin to gain a deeper understanding of what you do know. You become an increasingly active participant in determining how you understand the world. You also begin to develop a feeling for the truth of a situation or an idea as though thinking itself, when freed of the clutter, the debris, as it were, of other people's notions, begins to function as a new organ of perception, resonating with the validity or rightness of what it encounters.

Rudolf Steiner speaks emphatically about one aspect of this challenge: the teachings of a spiritual researcher or teacher are to be examined the most carefully of all.

*2) I shall never lose sight of the living obligation to constantly
increase the sum of my concepts and ideas.*

In other words: I will consciously practice the art of
learning. I will know myself to be a learner. There is nothing worse than getting stuck in a rigid set of ideas, no matter how good they might be. Even Anthroposophy. A limited set of ideas blinds me to the unexpected, the small
miracles that open up new dimensions of life. The learner
maintains an inner mobility or flexibility that opens him
or her to what is new in the world, to the seeds of change
and growth in one's surroundings. I first became aware of
the validity and the power of this as a practice through
teaching. The teacher/learner or learner/teacher is engaged
in an activity that places one in a state of intimate connectedness with one's pupils, whether children or adults. I
became ever more aware that learning is a spiritual activity. It is not about learning *something,* but rather about the
practice of widening one's relationship to the world. As my
soul becomes able to consciously embrace more and more
of the world I encounter, the forces of love come more
strongly to the forefront of my life. In learning, the forces
of love overcome those forces that sow fear and distrust in
the human soul.

In every moment, one has the opportunity to learn.
Recently I visited my friend Thomas in his workshop. He
was sanding a carefully crafted wooden fork. Smiling his
shy smile and looking just a bit sheepish he said quietly, "It
is for Jane. She likes to eat with wooden utensils. Just like a
little child." In that moment, I understood something about

Jane that I had previously not been aware of and found that my sense of who she is has just been enriched. And not only had I learned something about Jane, the love of little children for wooden things took on a slightly new significance for me. I realized that their enjoyment of a wooden spoon must rest on their ability to taste its authenticity. On top of this, I also learned something new about Thomas. He enjoys making Jane these small gifts. His enjoyment gives their marriage stability: joy creates strength.

Almost every moment of our lives are filled with lessons like this. The challenge is to notice them.

3) I can only know the truth of those things to which I am attached by neither sympathy nor antipathy.

In 1904, Rudolf Steiner published a book "depicting some portions of the supersensible world." The first chapter begins with a quote from Goethe:

> As soon as we become aware of the objects around us, we start to consider them in relationship to ourselves, and rightly so, because our fate depends entirely on whether they please or displease, attract or repel, help or harm us. This very natural way of looking at and assessing things appears to be as easy as it is necessary, yet it exposes us to thousands of errors that often put us to shame and make our lives miserable.
>
> We undertake a much harder task when, in our keen desire for knowledge, we strive to observe natural objects in and for themselves and in their relation-

ship to one another, for we soon feel the lack of the standard of liking and disliking, attraction and repulsion, usefulness and harmfulness, that came to our aid when we were considering objects in relationship to our human selves. We are forced to renounce this standard totally and, as dispassionate and quasi-divine beings, to seek out and examine what is, and not what pleases us. This means that neither the beauty nor the usefulness of any plant should move true botanists, who rather should study its morphology and its relationships to the rest of the plant kingdom. Just as the sun shines equally on all plants and entices them forth, so too should botanists observe and survey them all impartially, and take the data and standards for their assessment, not from the human domain, but from the domain of the things under observation.[29]

True understanding lies beyond the limitations of my personal inclinations, likes, and dislikes. In fact, any knowledge that is colored by personal preferences, likes and dislikes, or the restrictive qualities of preconceived notions, must be in some way limited, as it is colored through my own, necessarily partial, view of the world. Most important, those things that I view solely through the lens of my own subjectivity can do little to change me. By categorizing them according to my own inclinations, I rob them of their power to widen and deepen both my understanding of and relationship to the world around me.

29 Rudolf Steiner, *Theosophy*, pp. 21-22

For some, knowledge that is devoid of personal emotion is cold and impersonal. While this is certainly true of intellectual knowledge which leaves us on the outside looking in, it is not the case with the quality of understanding that awakens within us when we selflessly give something space within our soul and allow it to reveal to us its own true nature. When this happens, we discover a quality of emotion that surpasses anything personal. The light of true understanding is always imbued with the warmth of pure love. When experienced strongly enough, this warmth can move one to action.

The fourth rule or vow, and thus the last of the fundamental conditions for esoteric training, comes as a bit of a surprise. Yet although unexpected, it does lead us into the heart of the meditative work that follows:

4) I will strive to overcome my reservations towards what seems abstract.

One of the challenges Rudolf Steiner poses in his description of a path for the Western mind to conscious experience of the spirit is the challenge to liberate one's thinking from its accustomed dependence on the perceptible world and enable it to turn its attentiveness toward those realities not readily available to one's usual sense-bound thinking. This can only be achieved if one is willing to let go of what initially does give one's thought content a concrete anchor in the world. When I think about a tree, the presence of the tree in my consciousness serves to focus and guide my thinking. The richer and broader my experiences of trees are, the less likely my thinking is to go astray, and the more likely I am to come to an understanding of the relatedness that exists between trees, their environment, and so on. With some effort, I will be able to come to certain insights concerning the growth process of various trees, the fact that different trees have different needs in terms of water and light, that some trees are much loved by birds, and that others have a special relationship to ants or other insects. With time, I may gain an inkling of the gestural differences between various trees and a feel for qualitative differences between the nature of an oak tree, for instance, and a birch tree. Loving interest and scientific discipline can take me a long way toward an understanding of the nature of trees. But the very fact of the tree's concrete presence in the perceptible world stands between me and knowledge of the divine activity that realizes itself in the living tree.

To find a path to this quality of knowing, I must learn to see the tree not as it is, but as the image or picture of what brings it into being. I must allow the tree to become a symbol of something more powerful, more encompassing, more perfect than its apparent self. Only by overcoming my dedication to the tree's appearance can I allow it to become, as it were, transparent to the spiritual reality manifest in it.

The night before last we were blessed with a light snow. In the morning, everything was covered with an inch or so of pristine white. When I went out to the woodshed to get an armful of wood for the morning fire, I discovered an array of animal tracks. One of them was unfamiliar to me. At breakfast, I described them to my oldest daughter and son, both of whom had some experience with tracks. They too were puzzled. We all went out to look at them. After trying out different possibilities—perhaps a raccoon, or a possum—my son decided that the tracks belonged to a fisher. Someone went and got the field guide and sure enough, the tracks in the snow matched those depicted in the book. At this point, the children were satisfied and stories of fishers were recalled: Last summer one had played havoc with the neighbor's chickens, and I remembered coming across one during an early morning cross-country ski excursion years ago in Vermont.

We followed the tracks through the snow. They began on the porch by the front door, led out to the woodshed, then up through the garden to the duck shed. We could experience his movements, noticed where he had stopped, could picture him snuffling along outside the duck shed. The tracks directed our attention to the creature that had left them behind. It would make no sense to think of them as a reality unto themselves. Only if one is able to let the tracks lead his consciousness to the animal that made them do the tracks have any meaning.

This process of the emancipation of thinking from the bonds of the perceptible world can be supported by learning to focus one's thinking on concepts that come to expression in the sense world only in various degrees of approximation. In his commentary to this fourth "rule," Rudolf Steiner calls attention to two things: the first are geometrical concepts, such as a circle, the second are high moral ideals, such as love and kindness. Neither come to expression in the world of percepts in their full perfection; one can only experience them fully by liberating them from the specific instance and allowing them to express themselves contemplatively.

The practice of anthroposophy starts with these six exercises and the striving to live in accordance with the four "rules" or vows. Together they serve to bring calmness to the soul, while at the same time opening it to what life has to offer. They are a source of inner strength and resiliency. Working with them quiets one. You become less talkative, more attentive. You learn to listen. Within you grows a space of inner peace, and you become less inclined to be unduly affected by the ups and downs of life. They lead to a living sense of centeredness and presence, and are an ongoing source of inner health.

VII.   Slowing Down

This was sheer idleness to my fellow-townsmen, no
doubt, but if the birds and flowers had tried me by
their standard, I should not have been found wanting.

Henry David Thoreau

The first time Rudolf Steiner published a description
of the inner path that forms the foundation of anthroposophical practice was in a series of articles for the Theosophical magazine *Luzifer.* A collection of these articles was
later published as *How to Know Higher Worlds.* The book
unfolds in a wonderful sequence of exercises and experiences, that, as Arthur Zajonc wrote in the foreword to the
1994 English edition, "chart[s] a meditative path that leads
both to inner peace and to enhanced powers of the soul
and finally to the lifting of that veil that separates us from
spiritual knowledge." In his words, it is a path "through self-
knowledge to compassionate action in the world."[30]

This is not, however, a straight or linear path. It winds
through life, now in light, now in darkness. It circles round
to meet itself. Each meeting is fraught with the newness

---

30   Arthur Zajonc, in Rudolf Steiner, *How to Know Higher Worlds*

of an ever-broadening vista. The path has it own rhyt.
its cycles, its moments of expansion and contraction. 1
cyclicity is organic and deeply intertwined with the life of
the individual soul. It is progressive yet returns always to its
origin, spiraling out from where it both set out and arrives.

As with a multi-colored braid, one can discover and follow certain threads or themes as they weave in and out
of sight. One of these, I believe, must be addressed much
more consciously today than when Rudolf Steiner was
writing. It is a theme that is present throughout most of
the book, although it is rarely spoken of explicitly. When
he does so, Steiner speaks of it in relation to the practice of
patience: none of the exercises he describes lead to immediate results. When done with a gentle, steady patience, they
bring forth new capacities, which arise as though of themselves. Nothing can be forced; nothing can be hurried. As
with the growth of a plant, each change in the nature of
one's consciousness will appear when the time is right. The
quality of patience that Rudolf Steiner speaks of in relation
to the exercises he describes is an inner mood of expectant
restraint. It is imbued with a chaste hopefulness, nothing
grasping or selfish. It is a humble patience.

Life today does not leave much space for patience of any
sort. It hurries us along from one thing to the next, often
leaving us feeling harried and constantly behind. There
simply isn't time to be patient. Anyone wishing to learn
patience in this fast-paced world must do so consciously.

The first step lies in learning to slow down. Stop

hurrying. Don't let yourself be rushed along from one thing to another. Learn to take your time, savor things, enjoy what life has to offer. Be attentive to the unexpected.

Many people today when hearing this say something along the lines of: "Sounds great. But where will I find the time to slow down between my work, my children, my friends. Just keeping everything afloat takes every minute of my time. And at the end of the day, I still haven't finished everything I should have."

I know the feeling all too well. When I was teaching full-time, with young children at home, and still traveling to work with schools both in the United States and abroad, I could literally feel the weight of everything I wasn't getting done, although I was leading an almost monastic, focused life. The things undone and the things that were somehow getting done on the fly lurked constantly in the shadows. Whenever I stopped to simply breathe out, I could hear them there, crying out for attention. With time they began to take over my life. I felt as though I needed to hide from all the things I should be doing or should have done, and began to have a continuous feeling of guilt, as well as shame. And strangely enough, I found myself wasting time rather than tackling what was waiting to be done. Struggling to keep all the balls in the air was actually rather exhilarating. Looking back, I can say without hesitation that it gave me an artificially heightened sense of my own being and importance.

Something happened that enabled me to see what I was

doing in a new light. I took a hiking trip with a friend in the Swiss Alps. We searched for quartz crystals, climbing above the tree line and camping in the high alpine meadows. My friend, Urs, was a teacher, as I was. But he taught young children, whereas I have always taught adolescents and high school students. We didn't talk a lot as we worked our way through the scree and up the weather-worn rock faces. The silence was companionable. By the end of the first day, I realized that he had a very different approach to searching through the rocks than I did. He would start at the bottom and just slowly wander up, sometimes stopping to look more closely, or crouching down to dig a bit. I zigged and zagged across the slope, exploring whatever caught my fancy, staying at the promising spots longer before moving on again. Urs just poked his way up the slope, paying attention, it seemed, to everything that was there in front of him. Promising or not, the stones interested him. He loved touching them, weighing them in his hands. And amidst the rubble, he discovered the gems. One after another, he picked crystals out of the debris on the hillside.

Urs comes from Bern, a Swiss canton that is known for its slowness. There are jokes about it. The Bernese are so slow, they have to worry about snails in the fast lane. But watching Urs pick his way up the slope, I began to understand the importance of slowness. Busyness tends to be reactive; slowness has an inner gesture of responsiveness. Moving quickly through the world, I tend to pick out the things I hope to find rather than discover the riddles and opportunities the world has to offer in any given situation.

Slowness alone is, of course, not the answer. It is slowness permeated with interest or attentiveness. We might call it carefulness, in the sense of a relationship to the world that is full of caring. Especially for the little things. We are often exhorted to turn our attention to big things: great ideals or tasks. These are the things that keep us moving, ideals that draw us towards them, awaken in us the urge to become better, to develop further. They always exist in the future as something we are moving toward. Paying attention to the little things grounds us in the present, lets us be present in the present. The more I am able to imbue my attentiveness to what is here with me now with qualities of wonder and reverence, the richer and more revealing each moment becomes. Only so am I able to, as the poet says, hold "eternity in an hour."

One of the most noteworthy books of the last decades is a novel inspired by the life of the polar explorer John Franklin, called *The Discovery of Slowness*. The author, Sten Nadolny, gives a wonderfully gripping account of the world as experienced by an individual who is born slow, yet goes on to draw from his slowness a depth of perception and resolution that would enable him to become one of the most renowned seafarers of his time. The story is fictional, a lyrical tale crafted by a wonderfully imaginative author and woven around the threads of Franklin's life. Reading it, one gains a sense of experienced time, not the evenly measured ticking away of the clock or the accelerated abstraction that dictates so much of modern life. Time as experience. The pulse-beat of experience. At one point Nadolny's Franklin notes in his journal: "There are two points in time: a correct time and a missed time."[31] Some months later, when sitting in the school jail, a bare solitary cell, he muses: "There are three points in time: a correct time, a missed time, and a premature time."[32] The challenge we face today is to learn to wait for the right time, while remaining awake enough to recognize it and act in accordance with what is needed.

The ancient Greeks had a name for this quality of timeliness. They called it *kairos*, differentiating it from the flow of historical or sequential time they named *kronos*. The modern seeker is confronted with the challenge of developing a kairos consciousness, an attentiveness that is able to transcend the outer pressures of a culture of acceleration and recognize what is needed now, in this moment, in this situation.

How do you go about slowing yourself down? Incrementally. And by turning your attention to the things around you. The more you notice them, the more interesting they become. The more interesting they become, the more strongly you will feel the desire to linger with them. This desire to linger is what you must strive to awaken within your soul. How do you slow down? Learn to linger. Leave the house five minutes earlier than you have to and spend these five minutes taking note of the landscape you pass through on the way to your car, to the bus, or to the train. For these five minutes give your attention completely

---

31   Sten Nadolny, *The Discovery of Slowness,* p. 30
32   Ibid., p.33

to the world around you. Live into its details, notice what is always there around you. Some of it is beautiful, some less so. But it is all noteworthy.

If you can make this a daily practice, you may begin to notice yourself lingering with a clear conscience at other times during the day. The world as a whole begins to become more interesting. Some of your own hopes and fears, predilections and opinions may even begin to appear a bit tawdry in light of the discoveries there to be made.

It is possible to deepen the capacity to linger attentively into a capacity for creative receptivity. This can be done by intentionally practicing restraint. Restraint can be practiced in almost any circumstance. You can do it in social settings, or you can do it in ways that relate to your own private wishes and desires. It is best to do it with seemingly little things. And it is best to do it for the pure joy of doing, rather than for any anticipated result. Are you used to drinking a large coffee each morning? You might decide for the next week or so to drink only a small one instead. One can also choose to give up what one most likes for a period of time. The key is to do it playfully—seriously playfully, with the kind of earnestness a small child brings to his or her play. This kind of practice—the setting of challenges that have no direct relationship to anything outside myself, but are focused entirely on the way my "inner" life relates to the "outer" world—can be said to be the true play of the adult.

Practicing restraint in social contexts can open entirely new perspectives on the way in which each of our lives is interwoven with those around us. Do you tend to be the one who always has to have the last word in a discussion? Choose to refrain from doing so. Are you most comfortable guiding the course of a social process? Let someone else take the lead. Hold yourself back from answering questions. Practice restraint. You might be surprised at what you discover.

Slowing down does not simply mean going more slowly. By holding back you also open a space for something new to happen, for the seeds stirring in the soul to grow and bear fruit. Slowing down is a gentle thing. The gentleness it engenders within appears mirrored in the world around. Small, tender things begin to appear. Learning to slow oneself is a process of gentling the soul. Like a well-gentled horse, it loses its skittishness, and the strength that lies in its depths flows forth. The gentled soul is a powerful soul.

The practices of intentional lingering and consciously choosing moments of restraint can be turned inward. When brought to bear on a purely spiritual or ideal content, they provide firm footing for a healthy meditative practice.

VIII.   Silence

Let us be silent, that we may hear the whisper of God.

Ralph Waldo Emerson

Years ago my friend Nate returned from a tour of duty in Vietnam badly shaken by his experiences there. For many months he was unable to speak of what he had seen and heard. He stayed away from people, seeking solace in the woods and fields surrounding his mother's home. It was a difficult time, both for him and for those closest to him. His experiences had left him deeply wounded and quite unable to come to terms with the realities of life without the constant presence of fear and imminent death. He had been in the infantry, a scout able to move silently through the jungle. He had watched his closest comrades cut down by sniper bullets and carefully concealed traps laid across the narrow jungle paths. He had learned to know a silence fraught with danger, ready to explode in any moment into a cacophony of destruction.

One evening, during one of his recurring struggles with the inner demons these experiences had called to life within him, I went in search of him and found him squatting in a copse of birch trees overlooking a small sheltered valley. It was a peaceful place, quiet in the soft light of the fading day. I watched him, not speaking, and knew that the outer peace was in stark contrast to the turmoil in his soul.

He had the ability to squat without moving for long periods. I settled in beside him and waited. Daylight faded and darkness came. The woods grew quiet, then the noises of the night began: the hum of insects, the cadence of the frogs in the marshland by the creek. I fought back every urge to speak to him and waited, looking out into the night.

I don't know how long we stayed there, silent under the birch trees. He didn't stir until the moon rose above the hills opposite us. He reached out and took my hand, holding it like a little child holds the hand of a big brother or sister. Through the darkness, I could feel his eyes upon mine and knew that he was crying, the tears welling up and rolling silently down his cheeks.

After awhile, he let go of my hand, rose to his feet in one silent fluid motion and set off through the woods towards home. I rose, somewhat more stiffly, and followed him.

We spoke only once about that night. It was some months later, the summer was gone and the chill of autumn was in the air. We sat again in the darkness with only the light of the woodstove. He told me how he had tried to find peace and some kind of inner quiet. Yet each time the memories flooded back, the fear, the callousness, the scream of a rocket appearing out of the impenetrable green, the terror on the faces of fellow soldiers. These memories were much worse for him than the actual experience had been as they repeated themselves again and again, and there was nothing that he could do. Although he was afraid of them, he also knew that the only way to put them to rest was to face them and struggle with them. He said that if he couldn't conquer them he would never be free of them. He had been in the midst of such a struggle when I found him there by the birch trees that night. My silence had been more powerful even than the peacefulness of the setting. For the first time, he had brought his demons to rest.

It was by no means the end of his struggles. He died in a motorcycle accident five years later after having spent time in and out of psychiatric care. But for that one night, he had felt the power of silence.

Inner peace, inner quiet, intentional silence is something one must attain before any meditative path can begin to lead to true experience. Coming to silence is something each of us must learn. It is only in silence that the spirit can be heard.

Silence is rare in today's world. We are constantly bombarded by noise, sometimes to the extent that some people feel uncomfortable when it is missing. The lack of outer silence or stillness makes finding inner silence, inner stillness, more challenging. Yet anyone wishing to earnestly cultivate a meditative path must learn to open an inner space of silence.

Finding balance is one of the first steps towards opening the capacity for silence within yourself. When you begin to explore the nature of balance, you discover quite quickly that balancing is a dynamic undertaking. Place your feet together and stand with your eyes closed. Observe how you are in constant motion. You weave backwards and forwards, side to side. These are minimal movements, gentle and usually unconscious. But in every moment when you are standing or sitting upright you are engaged in this dynamic process of finding your center. Balancing is the ongoing creation of your individual center.

You can work consciously to enhance your sense of balance. A simple way to do this is to make yourself a balance beam and spend a few minutes a day on it over the course of several weeks. Begin simply, learning to walk the beam forwards and backwards. When you are able to do this fluidly with your arms hanging loosely by your side, slow down. Take each step consciously, experiencing inwardly the act of maintaining your balance, while at the same time holding yourself back. With practice, you can learn to slow your passage along the beam until you are fully immersed in the act of balancing. You come to experience what Phillipe Petit characterized as a force streaming upward from the center of his being, overcoming everything that would drag him down.

In this upward streaming, you can discover another aspect of the nature of your self. Here it reveals itself as a dynamic force, a force of levity and responsiveness, weaving constantly in and through the forces of gravity. The more you are able to master the art of balancing the more deeply you become aware of the fluid, mobile nature of this inner stream. It is never rigid, never static. It moves with and in relation to the world around it. Under normal circumstances, it is always there, always present, like an eternal spring.

Learn to experience it coursing not only through your body but also through your soul. Stay conscious of its presence: when you are working alone, in your meetings with other people, in those moments when events threaten to throw you out-of-kilter, to push you off-balance. Remind yourself that within you springs forth a stream of gentle, quiet responsiveness that never goes dry. It is always there. It was there before you were born, it is there in every moment of your life, and it will continue on its journey when you lay this earthly body aside. This never-ceasing stream is you. Only in it can you find the capacity of silence, of stillness.

For most of us, finding silence is not something that comes naturally. We have to work at it. Practicing silence is as much a choice as choosing to practice an instrument or to memorize poetry. It takes practice and repetition.

One way to begin is to find a quiet place in nature and sit quietly. Don't think about anything. Just let the natural world take you up in its embrace. Begin small. Try to be absolutely silent for two minutes, then five minutes a day. Let the sounds of the world pass over the calm waters of your soul like a breeze over the surface of the water. Gently restrain the inner voice, the chattering of your soul. Simply be quiet. Neither listen nor not listen, neither see nor not see. Strive to feel only quietness and peacefulness. Slowly increase the amount of time you spend in this state, but don't become too enamored of it. Here, too, balance is important.

It is also possible to practice silence in the stream of daily life. A very fruitful exercise is to restrain yourself from speaking without withdrawing from a conversation. Strive to remain inwardly involved in the flow, but refrain from voicing your own opinions. This practice can be expanded upon if your social or vocational setting is supportive. The practice of maintaining silence for periods of each day or for a day each week is a source of empathetic strength. With some tact, it is possible in most settings. There have been periods in my teaching career when I have maintained silence one day a week with full (although initially reluctant) support of both my students and colleagues.

For the meditant, silence is not the absence of sound, but rather a state of soul. As the soul grows silent, the sounds of the world become more varied and expressive. Silence is the quieting of soul noise, not world noise. I meet regularly with a small circle of friends to work collaboratively on a series of meditative verses that Rudolf Steiner gave toward the very end of his life. These meetings take place in one corner of a large, open-plan kitchen-dining-living room. There are others in the house and while they are respectful of the nature of our work and the need for quiet, there are moments when one or the other must pass through the space. At the beginning of each session, such intrusions disturb the flow of the work. It feels as though we can't find the right quality of silence to immerse ourselves in the content of the meditation. My first inclination was to change the venue of our meetings to a location blessed with the kind of stillness we seek in meditation. Outer quiet does, at times, make attaining inner quiet easier. But then, I considered the way the evenings had unfolded. We had to make an extra inner effort to focus ourselves. By doing so, we overcame any lingering sense of laziness and gave ourselves more fully to the process. Interestingly, this enhanced quality of focus was, for me, combined with a strong sense of empathetic acceptance of the others in the house who still had to go about the important business of their lives. These two soul activities, working each in conjunction with the other, brought about a new quality of silence that grew up about us in a gentle, accepting manner and allowed the meditative work to find its true place within the living reality of this household.

I have come to believe strongly that this is where meditation and meditative work has its true home: the esoteric reality of one's life is to be found and practiced within the exoteric reality. There is no longer the possibility to retreat from life in order to find the spirit. We must take our meditative practice into our daily lives and let each enrich the other.

Among the most intense spiritual dialogues I participate in presently are those with my friend and colleague Chris Bamford. These often take place at a small diner in the village of Copake, New York, against a background of popular music of the 1960s and the buzz of the local lunch crowd. We are now fairly well known there, the staff is friendly and leaves us pretty much alone. Our dialogues are unplanned; we begin with whatever questions or thoughts we've been working with, listen to one another, question, ponder and slowly, carefully feel our ways to deeper understanding. As the dialogue progresses, the noises around us disappear and a quality of silence embraces us, grows around us. This silence is palpable. It is a silence of attentiveness and responsiveness. It is a space of silence woven of the threads of spiritual activity. Within this space, things happen.

Mastering the art of creating silence is an essential aspect of the practice of anthroposophy. It is the foundation of all soul receptivity—both in daily life and in meditation. The unquiet soul, caught up in its busyness, in its trials and tribulations, in its accomplishments and dreams, can never move beyond itself. The soul that is able to quiet itself and, by doing so, open a space of receptive silence, finds itself immersed in a world of previously unimagined possibilities of growth and transformation.

IX. Studying Steiner as a Contemplative Practice

We approach the things of the supersensible world with the right attitude if we take it as a given that sound thinking and perception are capable of understanding all true knowledge that can flow toward us from the higher worlds. We should also recognize that by taking this kind of understanding as our starting point and laying a firm foundation with it, we are taking a great and important first step toward higher seeing for ourselves...

Rudolf Steiner

As one step toward attaining an experienced knowledge of the spiritual dimensions of reality, Rudolf Steiner called attention to the importance of the study of spiritual writings, both his own and those of others. He spoke about the significance of such study and the role it plays in creating a basis for conscious spiritual experience. He gave his own students of meditation specific books to work with and expected them to devote at least a half an hour each day to their study. He emphasized that through study it is possible to attain an understanding of the nature of the spiritual before one has acquired the ability to be consciously aware of the presence of the spiritual in one's own experience of the world. Study also opens one's mind to the possibility of the spiritual, making its presence easier to recognize.

Among the great spiritual texts of Western civilization is a poem by the 13th century Florentine poet Dante Alighieri. Originally titled *The Comedy of Dante Alighieri*, it is known today as *The Divine Comedy* and tells of Dante's journey through Hell (Inferno) and Purgatory before finally arriving at the gates of Paradise. As with much medieval poetry, the poem is rich in imagery, both historical and mythological, and a masterpiece of the use of imagery in a symbolic and allegorical manner. Hidden in the imagery of Canto IX, following the appearance of the Erinnyes, crying out for Medusa, one finds the following: "O ye possessed of sturdy intellects, observe the teaching that is hidden here, beneath the veil of verses so obscure."

These oft quoted lines invoke the reader to see as it were through the symbolism with which the poet describes his experience of the first stage of the soul's journey after death, to glimpse what lies behind the "veil." Each image points toward a greater, more sublime truth. The awakened soul, the soul aware of the presence of higher forces in the unfolding of its life—in Dante's words: those of sturdy intellect—experienced these symbols and images deeply.

This changed over the centuries. We are not moved by such imagery in the same way. Symbols and allegories firmly anchored in a religious experience of the world do not have the same palpable presence for us as they did for those living some 700 years ago. We have become both more intellectual and less sensitive to what lies beyond the "veil."

For Steiner, study of the spiritual work of others was one step toward overcoming the barriers raised by the intellect and, by doing so, increasing again our sensitivity for what the intellect denies.

Steiner himself was a dedicated student. He took an active interest in the work of his predecessors and in that of his contemporaries, reading what they had written and living with their thoughts to the point that he was able to inwardly grasp the intentionality and conceptual experience from which they arose. In working with the thoughts of his fellows, he practiced an explicitly contemplative approach that allowed him to pass through the "veil" of their conclusions and supporting arguments, and to understand the nature of the conceptual context upon which they were based. He writes about this in the preface to the 1923 edition of *The Riddles of Philosophy*: "You are only then able to do justice to a world view, when you are able to immerse yourself in it entirely."[33]

Study, in Steiner's understanding, is not a question of interpretation and criticism or acclamation. It is a process of immersion, of giving oneself totally to the unfolding of another's thought, to the imagery, metaphors, and conceptual forms through which the thoughts are developed. One lives into what another has experienced through the way the experiences are brought to expression.

This act of living into and becoming intimately aware of

---

33   Rudolf Steiner, *The Riddles of Philosophy*, p. xvi

another individual's experience is an act of intellectual self-lessness. One learns to know the other from within rather than analyzing, interpreting, and critiquing from without.

Anyone who discovers an affinity for anthroposophy as a spiritual path will find ongoing study of Steiner's own works to be helpful. Studying Steiner is, in fact, an essential facet of the practice of anthroposophy.

It is, however, not an easy undertaking. Even those who are able to read him in the original German can attest to the difficulties he presents his readers. This difficulty is intensified when reading him in translation. He never intended to write in a way that would easily give the reader the illusion of spiritual experience. Such experience only has value when one comes to it through one's own effort. In the preface to *Theosophy*, his first book concerning the nature of the spiritual world, he wrote:

> This book cannot be read the way people ordinarily read books today. In some respects, its readers will have to work their way through each page and even each sentence the hard way. This was done deliberately; it is the only way this book can become what it is intended for the reader. Simply reading it through is as good as not reading it at all. The spiritual scientific truths it contains must be experienced; that is the only way they can be of any value.[34]

Working through Steiner's presentation deliberately, step by step, rethinking as it were the thoughts as they unfold,

---

34   Rudolf Steiner, *Theosophy*, p. 8

leads to an experience of what lies behind them. Only this experience is of value. The thoughts provide the medium within and through which the experience is possible. In order to arrive at the experience you must participate in the activity.

You must read Steiner slowly, a little bit at a time. He challenges us to practice what might be called a mantric approach: to let his way of unfolding a thought or developing an imagination guide and focus your own thinking. If you choose to embark on such a journey, with enough patience to not try to hurry things along by discarding what seems foreign or too outlandish and simply holding onto what is in some way familiar, you can come to an experience similar to that of perceiving the light at dawn. Relationships, details, colors, and shapes become apparent, which until then had been hidden in darkness.

Steiner thinks differently. Not only does he think different things: he thinks those different things differently. Studying Steiner is a step along the path of freeing your own thinking from its dependence on the perceptual side of the sense world. It is an exercise in the mobility or flexibility of thought. It is something like yoga for the mind.

There are, of course, anthroposophists who would cringe at such a comparison. Didn't Steiner speak clearly about the path of yoga being unsuited for modern consciousness? Yes he did. He also recommended meditating on verses from the *Bhagavad-Gita* and, toward the end of his life, spoke of a yoga of the senses. Rudolf Steiner was never dogmatic. Only followers can be dogmatic. Steiner always spoke within a discursive context. Each statement asks to be understood within that context. Friend and foe alike have done him a great disservice in bandying his statements about with little or no regard for the context within which they appear.

The indiscriminate use of decontextualized ideas is the antithesis of what Steiner seemed to have understood concerning the role his own work would play in the spiritual development of other individuals. He was certain that only through deliberate study could an individual find an independent, intentional relationship to insights into the nature of the spiritual. He viewed such study as a stimulus to greater spiritual awareness, as one of the practices that prepare the soul for conscious experience of spiritual reality.

The active mantric re-thinking or inner re-creation of Steiner's thought stimulates the soul in a variety of ways. First, there is the above-mentioned flexibility or mobility in thinking. This leads to a widening of one's conceptual horizons. If you are able to take the leap and overcome the urge to reject anything that doesn't fit in some way with what you already know and believe to be true, with what you have already learned and with what agrees in some way with conventional wisdom, if you can actively allow Steiner's thinking to guide you, you can experience that when viewed, as it were, from within, his thinking has an integral validity that opens new and previously unimaginable vistas.

The challenge is to be neither fascinated nor repulsed by the content of his thoughts. The fruits of the conscious practice of equanimity prove essential as a basis for productive study. The content is to some extent secondary. More important than the content is the tensile character of the thought process itself. It leads one into rather than away from the topic at hand.

As a general rule when working with any spiritual text, depth is more important than breadth. It is better to read one book by Steiner well than to read many superficially. Find a book or series of lectures that speaks to you. Often it will be something unexpected, a gift, a serendipitous find at a favorite bookstore, something someone mentions. One friend discovered Steiner while searching the do-it-yourself section of a used bookstore in Belgrade, Serbia. Among the various books on repairing computers, building staircases, weaving and pottery, he came across one entitled *How to Know Higher Worlds*. With it began a life journey that led among other things to our meeting years later at a picnic in California.

Go and find a book, or let the book find you, then befriend it. Learn to know it like you would a newfound friend. Perhaps you might read it through in one captivated night, skipping over the rough parts just to get a taste of what life has placed in your hands. Or you read a bit, then stop to think about it, laying the book aside until you are ready to go a step further.

However you do it, there is always a first time. Be gentle. Let the words, the thoughts, the imagery flow through you and wash over you. Don't be too critical, too analytical. That will come later. Try to simply get a feel for Steiner's approach, savor meaningful phrases; try to see the pictures he paints with words. When you have a feel for the whole, return to the beginning.

In my experience, it only makes sense to begin a systematic study of a text after I have acquired some idea of the whole. This is not only true of texts. If I set out to study dandelions, I won't begin in the laboratory or the library: I begin in a meadow. There I can encounter the dandelion in its living wholeness and in context. A Steiner text demands the same approach. It too is a living thing. Like an organism, each part has its meaning from the whole. Before getting too caught up in the parts, it is good to become acquainted with the whole.

But then, you must return to the beginning and work your way through deliberately, page by page, paragraph by paragraph, sentence by sentence. Sometimes word by word. You should embark on such a journey with the attitude: Nothing is unimportant; each little thing has significance. Sometimes even the choice of a preposition. The details are what bring Steiner to life, coaxing his writings back from the grey expanses of abstraction, giving them color and form, letting them speak.

There are many ways to begin such a study. I like to read a passage or a lecture a number of times, until I am able to rearticulate the whole thing in my own words. I will often do this with a piece of paper and pen at hand, and make short summaries in my own words of each paragraph. I don't expect to be able to recapitulate the text exactly, but well enough to gain a solid sense of the main topics; how Steiner moves from one to the other and the arcs or chains of thought throughout the text. In doing so, I come up against those moments or passages that 1) either challenge my ability to grasp the flow of thought or 2) have a special place in the flow of the text—passages or sentences that stand out or have a dramatic quality to them that sets them apart. The former I return to and work through more carefully, while the latter provide entry points into a meditative relationship with the text.

Sometimes it can take a long time for a passage to begin to make sense. The following is from the second lecture Rudolf Steiner gave to the first teachers of the Waldorf School in Stuttgart, Germany, shortly before the school opened in September 1919. It is the introductory lecture to a new approach to a psychological understanding of the human being, one that would lead to an understanding of human soul life in its relation to the entirety of the cosmos. He speaks of the pictorial character of a mental image, then says:

> Now when you consider the image character of mental picturing you must above all think of it qualitatively. You must consider its mobility, one might almost say its activity of being, but that might give too much the impression of being, of existence, and we must realize that even activity of thought is only an image activity. Everything which is purely movement in mental picturing is a movement of images. But images must be images of something; they cannot be merely images as such. If you think of the comparison of mirror images you can say to your-

selves: out of the mirror there appear mirror images, it is true, but what is in the mirror images is not behind the mirror, it exists independently somewhere else. It is of no consequence to the mirror what is to be reflected in it; all sorts of things can be reflected in it. When we have thus clearly grasped that the activity of mental picturing is of this image nature, we must next ask: of what is it an image? Naturally no outer science can tell us this, but only a science founded on Anthroposophy. Mental picturing is an image of all the experiences, which we go through before birth, or rather conception. You cannot arrive at a true understanding of it unless it is clear to you that you have gone through a life before birth, before conception. And just as ordinary mirror images arise spatially as mirror images, so your life between death and re-birth is reflected in your present life and this reflection is mental picturing. Thus when you look at it diagrammatically you must mentally picture the course of your life to be running between two horizontal lines bounded on the right and left by death and birth.

You must then further represent to yourself that mental picturing is continually playing in from the other side of birth and is reflected by the human being himself. And it is because the activity you accomplish in the spiritual world before birth or conception is reflected by your bodily nature that you experience mental picturing. For those able to truly understand, this activity is a proof, because it is an image, of life before birth.[35]

I first read this passage when I was 20 years old and a beginning teacher at a farm-based boarding school in Vermont. At that time, all I could do was shake my head. Since then, I have read the passage more times than I can remember, I have worked it through with students in teaching courses in Europe and America, and in workshops with teachers in various venues. Each time I return to it, I find something new to puzzle me. Strange as it may sound, this is one of those great things about studying Steiner: each time you think you have understood something, you discover something new about it. I can remember well the cry of delight from one participant in a workshop, when she discovered a "new" sentence in a lecture she had worked with off and on for almost thirty years! That sentence opened up a new dimension of the lecture for her.

The passage above can be summarized in a simple statement: Mental picturing is an image of what we experience before birth or conception. This sentence is in fact there in the passage, more or less in the middle. Leading up to it, Steiner characterizes mental imaging and illustrates certain aspects of it with the analogy of the mirror. Following it, he indicates briefly how it occurs ("And it is because the activity you accomplish in the spiritual world before birth or conception is reflected by your bodily nature that you experience mental picturing"), then points out that for anyone with the capacity for true understanding, this is

35   Rudolf Steiner, *Study of Man*, pp. 27-28

proof of life before birth. We meet the mirror both before and after the summarizing statement. At first, it is the familiar mirror on the wall that reflects whatever passes before it; later it becomes transformed into a mirroring process taking place in time through which pre-birth activity is transformed into the experience of mental picturing.

Based on a superficial reading of the passage you are faced with a choice: you can either accept Steiner's position or not. But neither is intellectually tenable: no one seeking to come to a true understanding of anything will be satisfied with simply accepting or rejecting something he or she does not understand. So, back to the beginning.

The previous paragraph in the lecture from which this passage was taken, concludes with the mental *picture*, this one begins with mental *picturing*. We are no longer concerned with the content of the mental pictures, but with the activity through which we form mental pictures. This activity is also an image, it points toward something just as the image in a mirror points toward what is reflected in it. If there were not something outside the mirror for the mirror to reflect, there would be no mirror image. The mirror, however, reflects anything visible that passes before it. There is a restrained selflessness about a good mirror. It neither chooses nor distorts what it reflects. Mirror images can also move. They do not move on their own accord: the movement we see in the mirror is the movement either of the object being reflected or of the mirror itself. In the latter case, we see objects moving across the face of the mirror although the objects themselves are at rest. In this context,

it is the apparent movement in the mirror image of a moving object upon which we should focus our attention. This
is movement, yet it is only the image of movement: a moving image. Such too is the nature of mental imaging. In it
we too find the reflection of movement, the reflection of
activity.

The activity of forming mental images is analogous to
the pictorial character of reflections in a mirror. (Steiner
uses an image—the mirror—to clarify the pictorial nature
of an activity.) If mental imaging has a reflective or pictorial
nature, then we must ask: Of what is it a picture?, because
no reflection or picture is a reality unto itself.

The first arc of thought in the passage concludes with
the question: of what is it [mental imaging] a picture?

The answer to this question leads us into what are for
most of us unknown realms. The statement: "Mental picturing is an image of all the experiences we go through
before birth, or rather conception," though formally an
appropriate response to the question, is more of a riddle
than a clarification. The attentive reader will recognize that
this statement changes the nature of the challenge. Up to
this point it is possible to follow Steiner's logic with what
we already "know" about mental pictures and picturing.
Now that changes. We find that we must expand the concept of "mental picture," and the activity through which
we form mental pictures, to include experiences that have
taken place in a state of existence of which we have no
immediate conscious experience. If someone were to ask
me at a party: "And what were your experiences like before

birth?" I would have a hard time giving them an authentic answer.

I think that statements like this one give us the truest experience of the nature of Rudolf Steiner's conceptual approach. It is a statement with immeasurable potential for contemplative exploration. If the statement is to make sense, each of its concepts and their relationship to one another must be re-thought and imbued with new meaning. Have I ever observed the process of forming a mental image? What do I actually know about mental images and mental imaging? What is the difference between a mental image and a thought? To what extent can I begin to form a mental image of what Steiner terms the "experiences we go through before birth or rather conception"?

The more deeply you contemplate these questions, the more apparent it becomes that this single sentence opens a completely new field of exploration. Rudolf Steiner's work is rich with such sentences. We can call them seed sentences. They sow questions, rather than deliver answers. If you let them take root within the living context of your soul, the questions grow, reaching out into the world in search of light. And, as Rilke pointed out, in time the world begins to answer. You begin to make observations and discover things that enrich and fill out the questions, giving them new contour and substance.

There are many ways to deepen your contemplative relationship to these seed sentences. A productive first step lies in enriching and broadening your concepts. To do this, you have to find a way to move beyond the narrow linearity of what Suzuki termed the "small mind," the mind caught up in what comes to it from outside. In the latter part of the passage quoted above (p. 108-10), we find opportunities or points of entry that help us begin to bring the statement into movement. They come in the form of what we would today call a visualization exercise. The mirror creates spatial images. To grasp the nature of mental picturing, we must enter the stream of time. Imagine your life unfolding between the two thresholds of birth and death. Imagine further that mental picturing is constantly flowing into your life from beyond the threshold of birth and being reflected through the nature of your own being. This stream is thus brought into consciousness, and one is able to experience mental picturing.

The initial, somewhat static, analogical relationship is brought into movement. The reflected, imaginal character of mental picturing comes to expression in the flow of time. If one lives carefully into the visualization, it becomes palpably apparent that time is spoken of here with a level of complexity that challenges conventional concepts. Pre-natal experience is constantly flowing into life between birth and death. This experience exists in a dimension of time that transcends historicity and can only be captured intuitively or poetically, in a mode of thinking that allows us to rise "from beholding the creature into beholding creation" and enables "our mortality [to catch] for a moment the music of the turning spheres."[36] It is the quality that exists in the opening lines of Blake's

36   Owen Barfield, *Poetic Diction*, p. 181

Auguries of Innocence or Wordsworth's *Intimations of Immortality*. We find ourselves in a realm of time or timelessness that knows no past or future, only the eternal present. The activity that flows out of this eternal presence is reflected into the stream of time from birth to death and becomes the source of our mental picturing.

It is possible to intensify the poetic or artistic experience of a text. To do so, you must bring your own artistic abilities to bear upon it. Or, in other words, intentionally shift your consciousness from resting upon a thinking guided by the logical relationships of earthly things to an imaginative thinking guided by the inner essential qualities of the ideas themselves. When doing this, it is good to proceed methodically, and not gallop off in flights of fancy or indulge yourself in the pleasurable subjectivity of associative figments. One needs a high level of attentiveness to come to an objective imagination. This takes discipline.

One approach entails condensing the text, in a series of steps, into a germinal poetic phrase, and then allowing it to blossom again into a well-articulated sentence or group of sentences.

First, you read the sentence. As a next step, you re-articulate the sentence in your own words—simply re-articulate it, don't try to interpret it. Make it yours; don't try to project yourself onto it. As a third step, do so again, trimming away any non-essentials. As a fourth step, capture the essence of the sentence in a short, pregnant phrase. The fifth step is again a sentence, the sixth step a picture, and to finish the process, you read the sentence again.

With the statement (p. 112) from above, the path might look something like this:

1. Mental picturing is an image of all the experiences, which we go through before birth or rather conception.

2. In my ability to form mental images, I find a reflection of what I experienced in life before birth.

3. The source of mental picturing is pre-birth experience.

4. world awareness—spirit life

5. Coming to consciousness of the world around me is the reflection of a spiritual activity or movement.

6. The water flows up the sloping sand, retreats; only the tracks remain.

7. Mental picturing is an image of all the experiences we go through before birth or conception.

As with every spiritual exercise, the visible (in this case, the seven groups of words) is of less importance than the invisible. What happens from one step to the next? The activity lies in the spaces in between. The empty spaces—the in-between spaces—are most important. Each of the seven expressions is a picture of the activity out of which it was formed.

You can turn your attention toward these in-between spaces. Capture them in a short poem, a Haiku perhaps or a series of rhyming couplets. Try to capture the movement, the gesture, the quality of life and light that live unspoken within them. On the wall above my desk hangs a multi-colored study of one of Rudolf Steiner's meditations done by a colleague during a summer retreat. The colors he chose and the transitions between them capture the mood or moods that lie behind and radiate through the lines of the meditation. We experience them as qualities of feeling as we allow our consciousness to move through and be moved by the meditation as it unfolds.

Such seed sentences in Steiner's work can also become the focus of one's meditative life. In this case, the work described above serves as the preparation for meditative immersion in the thought content expressed by the words. When taking this step, one can become aware of the thought reality toward which the words lead us. We find that this reality is much larger and more fluid than the ideas might appear to be when cognized solely within the limited framework of our own personal experience. In this sense, the path toward meditative immersion in a thought is a sequential liberation of the thought content from the limitations of our own conceptual frameworks. Step by step, we allow the concepts to express themselves in their own mobile, creative, interconnected vitality. Contemplation or contemplative deepening becomes the doorway to a meditative encounter.

This process of contemplative transformation of a thought is a key aspect of anthroposophical meditation and is one of the things that is specific to it. The contemplative process brings the soul into a creative, intentional activity and leads thinking consciousness to a point where it takes on an aesthetic or feeling quality. Through focused inner activity, thinking consciousness is brought into motion, liberated from the gray shadows of abstraction and imbued with qualities of experience we only otherwise encounter in the sense world. As it becomes alive within me, it calls forth an inner soul movement, which can only be experienced artistically; it is an aesthetic movement, which expresses itself as joy, as bliss, as compassion, as gravity, as earnestness, as reverence. When the thought has become pure feeling, one is ready to enter into a meditative state.

X.   The Meditative Path

Such exercises in inner meditation will in general have to be carried on for a long time before the student is able to perceive any results. What belongs unconditionally to spiritual training are: patience and perseverance.

Rudolf Steiner

The step from a contemplative state into a meditative state is one of intentional surrender. It is similar to the act of surrender that leads one through the veil of the percept to an experience of the creative will at work in the sense world. This step takes one across an existential threshold into an experienced reality from which one cannot return unchanged. It is a step not to be taken lightly.

Rudolf Steiner took on his first students of meditation within the framework of the Esoteric School of the Theosophical Society. In accordance with the customs of that school, students who applied for membership were asked to accept and live by certain rules. Although these rules were not "enforced," they did form the basis of the relationship between the spiritual teacher and the student. It was a relationship of mutual trust. The student sought out the teacher because of his or her trust in that individual's spiritual capacities; the teacher committed himself to accompanying the student's path trusting in the student's commitment to intentional practice as it was sketched out in the rules. This was not a form of administrative trust based on policies and principles. It went far beyond that and was rooted in the mutual recognition of the inner striving each was committing to, a quality of trust that welled forth from the inmost core of each one's being. You can catch glimpses of this deep trusting when a small child takes hold of your hand to balance across a log in the woods or when you fall asleep, trusting completely in the mysteries of life to bring you safely to the dawning of a new day. It is at once both existential and transcendent. The rules standing at the threshold of Steiner's meditative schooling belong to this realm of trusting.

Steiner required of his students that they dedicate themselves to specific practices over the course of each day. These comprise the meditative practice of anthroposophy as it began. Knowing about them may be of personal interest, but only by doing them can you begin to unlock the seed-like spiritual capacities resting in your soul. These rules guide you in beginning your day, punctuate the flow of the day, and accompany the daily transition from waking consciousness into sleep. Fulfilling them does not take much time: 45 minutes a day—three times 15 minutes—is sufficient. It is not the amount of time that is important, but the way one uses it. Spending just a few minutes immersed in a spiritual truth during the course of a busy day has a wonderfully rejuvenating effect on your own spirits.

The morning and evening exercises frame your waking day. One accompanies you as you enter into waking consciousness; the other guides you into the experiences of the night. Although the content of one's meditations are certain to change as one's life unfolds, marking these two transitions of consciousness remains a constant.

Each transition has a unique quality. We awaken out of darkness. We fall asleep into the darkness. Between them is light. What happens during the light, happens also in the light of our consciousness. What happens in the night, belongs to the realms of consciousness that lie beneath the threshold of waking. These are not readily accessible to waking consciousness. We are much more likely to be able to remember what we did on a given day many years ago than to remember what happened to us as we slept last night. Yet the amount of time we spend asleep spans roughly a third of our lives. A person's biography is comprised of periods of waking and sleeping; one follows the other. If one thinks of one's life as a stream, it is apparent that one becomes aware of this stream each morning upon awakening, then loses awareness of it each night when one falls asleep. The stream does not cease to flow when we sleep. We merely relinquish our awareness of its journey. From here it is only a small step to the realization that I don't cease to be in the night; I continue to grow and change. The thoughts and questions, hopes and fears that accompany me into the night are not the same in the morning. My inner being has not stood still overnight. I am able to see the world with fresh eyes and embrace its challenges with a rejuvenated soul.

The soul returns from the night refreshed. Meditation in the morning, while the experiences of the night still linger, strengthens this mood and enables it to live on into the day. Perhaps the archetypal meditation for the morning is one that Rudolf Steiner gave in his lectures for curative educators: "I am in God."[37] All that surrounds me is divine. I am immersed in the beauty and mystery of something much greater, more fully embracing than myself. But I too am part of this. The unity with the spirit, which refreshes the soul in the night, can live on in me throughout the day.

The approach of the night is quite different. Darkness falls upon the earth, blanketing it in mystery and promise. Crossing the threshold into sleep, I surrender myself to something much greater, more majestic than I am able to fathom. Even in these times of readily available scientific explanations for everything, when you stand beneath the grandeur of the star-lit night sky, you cannot help but be moved by the enormity and beauty of the expanse above you. The evening meditation prepares you to surrender yourself to the sublime majesty that comes here to expression. The challenge is to do so without losing the seed experiences of the day that has just passed. If not lost, they will begin to ripen and bear fruit in the journey of the soul through the night.

These seed experiences come in different forms. They may present themselves as gifts brought to you by the world: the joy of a small child, the beauty of the colors

---

37   Rudolf Steiner, *Education for Special Needs: The Curative Education Course*, Lecture 10

of a calendula and larkspur blossoming in proximity to one another, an act of kindness done by someone without thought of recompense. They may take the form of a riddle. They may come to meet you as the disappointment, anger, or frustration of another person. They may only be present in little things, hardly noticeable among all the important things. In fact, it is often the little things, the gentle things, the tender beginnings that mean the most.

One part of any evening meditation is thus a retrospective journey through the day that has just passed, beginning with the evening and working one's way back to the morning. Steiner challenged his students to let the day unfold itself backwards: the flow of time, the events, the encounters. I have found this to be a very difficult, yet rewarding practice. Imagine that you have just walked upstairs to your bedroom. Now imagine yourself walking up the stairs from the top downwards; not just walking down the stairs backwards: walking up the stairs from the top to the bottom. You live backwards through the unfolding of a deed to its inception. In your mind's eye, you let the day unfold itself from evening to morning. You must practice a lack of attachment to what has occurred: you see your successes without any feeling of satisfaction; you become aware of your failures without reprimanding yourself. The day becomes a great panorama in which certain things show themselves to be more prominent than others. Encounters you barely noticed during the day show themselves to be of note, while other things slip into the background.

Holding this as a wholeness in your soul, you can turn

toward the archetypal evening meditation: "In me is God."
The divine weaves its way through the encounters I have
as I go about my daily life. I can recognize this, affirm it
and bear it into my sleep life. The events of the day accompany me, not as irritants, keeping me awake, but as seeds to
further growth. Through the course of the night they are
clarified, illuminated and strengthened.

There are many variations on these two archetypal
meditative phrases. You can also develop your own as you
progress along the path, and in accordance with the tasks
you take on in life. As a teacher, I learned to bring specific
children to life in my consciousness before going to sleep.
These were children who in one way or another had raised
questions in me during the day.

Re-living your day each evening, letting it lead you
through each encounter back to the source, your awakening, helps create an inner stream of continuity in life. A boat
adrift is tossed by the seas and driven by the waves. Rais-
ing even the most meager of sails allows the crew to set a
course and steer the craft, to work with wind and current
toward a chosen goal.

Ongoing practice of these morning and evening meditations leads to the growing experience of a presence in your
life that is neither defined nor determined by the outer
exigencies of your existence. This presence flows through
life like a stream, drawing everything that happens to you
into a unified whole. Contemplation of this stream leads
one to an understanding of one's biography and holds the
key to self-knowledge.

The morning and evening meditations can be enhanced or strengthened through the intentional immersion in specific content or symbols. In the following, I am going to explore more deeply three meditations given by Rudolf Steiner at various times. The first was given in his book *An Outline of Occult Science,* the second in connection with the meditative sentences mentioned above, and the third to the teachers of the first Waldorf school. Each highlights a different aspect of Steiner's approach to meditative work and the relation between meditative immersion and the way you encounter the world in your daily life.

It is helpful to clarify the steps or stages of a meditation. Meditative experience is the fruit of a series of steps leading up to the immersion of the soul in a meditative content. 1) You must prepare yourself and find the necessary inner space to let go of outer distractions and demands. 2) You must re-focus your inner activity and turn toward the content you have chosen. 3) You must concentrate your entire being on that content. These first three stages free you from the outer realities of your life, enabling you to allow something else to enter into and fill your consciousness. In the first, the soul finds a place of quiet, then, from this quiet place, she opens herself, receptive with tender anticipation, and brings the full force of her attentiveness to bear on the content she has chosen. The inner movement is one that progresses from me towards something other than me. During these three stages, I am very aware of myself, as well as of the meditative content. My consciousness is awake— even highly awake—and focused in what we might call head-consciousness.

This begins to shift as one moves into the fourth stage. To achieve this step, I must allow my consciousness to expand. It embraces the content and enters into a contemplative dialogue with it. This dialogue moves, as it were, downward, and what has been to this point thought content begins to take on a feeling quality. My consciousness moves from the head towards the heart without losing any of its clarity. The content of my meditation begins to express itself as feeling. The inner dialogue becomes wordless. This fourth stage is one of intentional surrender of my own sense of self. In it, I am neither self nor not self, but self becoming non-self. It marks the shift in the inner experience of the self as being the point from which I examine and understand the world to an experience of self that is completely at one with and part of the world that exists beyond the limitations of conscious separation.

As the meditative content transforms from thought content to feeling experience, my soul responds with feelings of love and reverence, the fifth stage.

These I lay as a form of inner offering on the altar of the spirit. Through them I am able to enter into an experience of communion, of oneness with what has now come to spiritual life within the expanded vessel of my consciousness. At this, the sixth stage, I may achieve a meditative encounter. Does it always happen? No. Each time, you travel as far as you can towards this encounter. But the intimate, unveiled experience of non-separateness, the intuitive oneness with another spiritual being is a matter of grace. It is always a gift.

The final stage of this journey is the transition back to "normal" consciousness. This is marked by a feeling of peace and deep gratitude. No matter how far you have managed to travel along the road towards spirit encounter, it is always good to let it end in a deeply experienced moment of gratitude. In my own practice, I have found that this gratitude can be allowed to flow forth not only to the spirit presence I have been allowed to approach, but also to all those who make this striving possible. One lets oneself simply be filled with gratitude.

There is an archetypal quality to these seven stages, occurring as they do within a single stream. Rudolf Steiner returned to it often over the course of his life. In general, we find a movement that takes us from one experience of consciousness to another. In the first stages we place ourselves intentionally and intensively in a new relationship to something, in the final stages we find ourselves touched or moved by it. The middle marks a turning point.

In the period from 1913 to 1922, Rudolf Steiner was engaged in crafting a building that would both house the anthroposophical movement and bring to artistic expression what anthroposophy strove to be. This building, the first Goetheanum, burned to the ground on New Year's Eve 1922/23. At the heart of the Goetheanum were a large auditorium and stage. They took the form of two interpenetrating circular spaces, roofed by two interpenetrating domes. The domes were supported by a series of pillars—fourteen in the auditorium, another twelve encircling the stage. The fourteen in the auditorium mirrored one another, forming two series of seven. The capitals and bases of the columns were carved as was the architrave connecting the capitals. In these forms and the connecting architrave, Rudolf Steiner brought this seven-fold developmental movement to artistic expression. For anyone wishing to gain a deeper understanding of anthroposophical meditation and the path of inner development with which it is intimately connected, a contemplative study of these forms is highly rewarding. Working with them artistically opens entirely new aspects of meditative experience.[38]

Steiner also spoke about these forms in relation to the path he described as a modern path of initiation, the meditative practice of anthroposophy. What you wrestle with most on this path are your own will forces. These go through a process of transformation as you proceed, becoming step by step less self-centered and more world-centered. This intentional metamorphosis of the up-swelling stream of creativity we experience as the will leads to the blossoming of selfless action without negating the spiritual presence of the I. Step by step, I awaken within myself the capacity to give of myself freely.

Let us turn our attention again to the content of meditation. This is only limited by your power of imagination. Depending on your temperament and inclinations, you can draw on the entire wealth of spiritual content from down

38 Information on the forms of the first Goetheanum can be found in Carl Kemper, *Der Bau* and in Rudolf Steiner, *The Goetheanum Building*. Heinz Zimmermann worked intensively with the seven-fold metamorphosis of the columns and their relationship with thinking and to group decision-finding processes.

through the ages, you can draw on the contents of Steiner's lectures, you can work with specific meditations that he has described in various books and lectures. What you choose is not as important as how you work with it. That said, there is little question that some content is more potent than others.

Rudolf Steiner introduced his listeners and readers to different forms of meditative content. These include imaginations or visualizations, mantric sentences, mantric verses, and symbols or, in German, *Sinnbilder*. These are spread throughout his work and often reflect the specific themes he was working on at the time, as well as the specific group of people he was working with. Anyone embarking on a meditative path today must find those that seem right for him or her. You may work with different ones at different periods of your life; you may live with a single one for many years. What is important is to remain honest with yourself and open enough to recognize when a meditation has ceased to be alive for you. Repeating a meditation out of pure habit can be counterproductive. There are very few teachers today who can lead you selflessly along the inner path. Each of us must learn to listen to his or her inner development and strive to stay awake enough to make the necessary adjustments or changes to his or her practice.

Imaginative Cognition

The anthroposophical path differs from other paths in that all of Rudolf Steiner's meditative teachings focus on awakening and strengthening the living power of thought within the soul. Together they comprise a comprehensive path of the transformation of consciousness. In one way or another, each of Steiner's meditations begins in full consciousness and leads to both a widening and a deepening of your conscious experience. In the process, you become aware of an inner source of activity, a presence within the soul that had previously been hidden behind the veil of what we know as our waking or thinking consciousness. The emergent presence of this source of activity in the weaving of consciousness is what Steiner spoke of as the birth of a new or higher self in the soul. Early on in his work he stressed the relationship between this emergent presence and the practice of imaginative cognition.

He introduced this practice in a series of visualization exercises. These visualizations begin with things you are familiar with from the sense world: stones, seeds, flowers, animals, etc. To do these exercises, you must have spent time with the objects or organisms, observing them and becoming aware of their singularities, of what makes them unique. The exercises prove themselves to be less than satisfying if you start with only an abstract idea of an object. To begin with, you form an inner image of, for example, a plant and an animal, perhaps a dandelion and a squirrel. Let these inner images be as vivid as possible. At first this may be difficult, but with practice you should be able to bring forth vivid, lively images through the powers of your imagination. Initially, these images will be influenced to a greater or lesser extent by your memories of specific dandelions and squirrels, and embedded in the context in which these memories were formed. Part of the challenge of these visualization practices is to free your inner image of the object from the influence of specific memories, thus coming to an objective inner experience of it.

The next step consists in bringing, in this case, the dandelion and the squirrel into relation with one another, to compare one with the other. I picture the dandelion in the middle of the newly greening meadow, the rosette of leaves still hugging the ground. Then I watch the leaves arcing up and out with the stalk stretching up between them bearing the yet un-opened bud up towards the light. The squirrel springs from place to place, scurrying up one tree, leaping from branch to branch then down another tree. Rarely does it come to rest, and then only briefly before it once again is on the move. The movement of the dandelion is outwards and upwards, one unified gesture that culminates in the wafting away of the seeds upon the wind. The squirrel moves here and there, up and down, leaping along in a fluid, wave-like motion. How different the qualities of their respective movements are. The dandelion remains rooted in the earth, reaching out and up into the air and the light. The squirrel is moved by something inside. It moves through its environment, seeking nuts and seeds, unearthing last year's stores, playing with other squirrels in mad dances up and down neighboring trees. How different, too, the forms of this plant and this animal.

Step by step, I bring the differences to consciousness, pondering them and contemplating what speaks through them. With complete attentiveness, I immerse myself in this activity. I become aware that each awakens different feelings in me. The dandelion streams forth a feeling that could perhaps be called joyful devotion. The feelings connected with the presence of the squirrel in my consciousness are more difficult to put into words. They are complex and touch me in a deeper way. Only after time do they coalesce into something clearer and more easily articulated.

I have done this and similar exercises for many years now. Over time the feelings called forth in the soul by the contemplation of plant and animal, of dandelion and squirrel, grow stronger. Their presence in my soul has changed the way I encounter the world. They have blossomed into an empathetic respect for the natural world and a sympathetic receptivity for what lies behind the words and gestures of other human beings. I find myself listening more deeply and with greater tolerance than I was once able to. I experience a lingering sadness when in social intercourse it proves impossible to pierce the brittle veneer of conventional superficiality.

The presence of such feelings in the soul, feelings that arise as the result of a focused, objective imaginative process, opens a new dimension of the world. One becomes increasingly aware not of appearances, but of the inner nature of the things themselves. How beautiful it is when these form a harmonious whole!

The Rose Cross Meditation

Somewhat later in his work, Rudolf Steiner introduces us to another, more elaborate visualization process. This one culminates in a meditative symbol. It is given here in its entirety.

> [...]we visualize a plant as it roots in the earth, as leaf by leaf it sprouts forth and unfolds its blossom. And now we place a human being beside this plant. We bring to life the thought of how the human being has characteristics and faculties which—when compared to the plant—may be considered more perfect than the plant. We contemplate how, according to his feelings and his will, he is able to move hither and thither, while the plant remains rooted in the earth. We let the thought unfold: Yes, the human being is indeed more perfect than the plant, but he shows peculiarities that are not to be found in the plant. Because they are not present in the plant, the latter may appear to us in some ways more perfect than the human being, who is filled with desire and passion and allows them to color his conduct. We see that the plant follows the pure laws of growth from leaf to leaf, that it opens its blossom passionless to the chaste rays of the sun. We may say more: the human being has reached a higher state of development than the plant; but he has purchased this perfection at the price of permitting his instincts, desires and passions to enter into his nature in addition to the forces present in the plant, which appear pure to us. We may now visualize how the green sap flows through the plant as an expression of the pure, passionless laws of growth. And we may then visualize how the red blood flows through the human veins and how it

is the expression of the instincts, desires and passions. These thoughts we bring to life in our souls. Then we visualize further how the human being is capable of evolution; how he may purify and cleanse his instincts and passions through his higher soul powers. We visualize how, as a result of this, something base in these instincts and desires is destroyed and how the latter are reborn upon a higher plane. Then the blood may be conceived as the expression of the purified and cleansed instincts and passions. In my thoughts I look now, for example, upon the rose and say: I see the green sap of the rose plant transformed into red; and the red rose, like the green leaf, follows the pure, passionless laws of growth. The red of the rose may now become the symbol of the blood as an expression of the purified instincts and passions which have been stripped of all that is base, and in their purity resemble the forces which are active in the red rose. We now seek to not only imbue our intellect with such thoughts but also to bring them to life in our feelings. We may have a feeling of bliss when we think of the purity and passionlessness of the growing plant; we can produce within ourselves the feeling of how certain higher perfections must be purchased through the acquirement of instincts and desires. This can then transform the feeling of bliss, which we had felt previously, into a feeling of gravity; and then a feeling of liberating joy may stir in us, when we surrender ourselves to the thought of the red blood which, like the red sap of the rose, may become the bearer of inwardly pure experiences. It is of importance that we do not confront the thoughts with which we form and give meaning to an image without feeling. After we have immersed ourselves in these thoughts and feelings, we transform them into the following image. Imagine a black cross. This is the image of the now destroyed lower drives and passions; where the two bars of the cross intersect imagine a circle of seven bright red roses. These roses are an image of the blood, which signifies the purified passions and desires.[39]

This soul exercise takes us through a process in which contemplative activity interweaves with picture-forming activity. We begin with a visualization: the forming of an inner picture of the growing plant, then placing beside it the inner image of a human being. These we contemplate, engaging in a thought process that leads to an opening of the idea of perfection with regard to the chaste lawfulness of plant growth in comparison to the subjective impulsiveness of human desires, drives and passions. This leads us to the forming of an imagination that moves beyond the boundaries of the sense-world: both the green sap of the plant and the red blood of the human being take on new meaning in this inner picture. The green sap of the plant becomes the image of the plant's purity; the red blood the image of personal desire and passion. We let these two, with meaning imbued images, come to life within us. We are fully conscious; our consciousness is immersed in the

---

39　Rudolf Steiner, *An Outline of Occult Science,* pp. 230-232

pure, gentle, even flow of the plant's sap, cast in a hue of green, and in the red-hued pulsing of the impatient human blood. Our thoughts become tinged with the innocent purity of the green, the passionate pulsing of the red. They take on an aesthetic quality, become richer and more alive within us. We take them a step further. The human being can change, can evolve into something that he or she has not yet attained. In the course of this transformation, the human being comes into a new relationship with the forces pulsing through his or her blood. These are purified. This path of thought, embedded as it is in the aesthetic experience of the flow of life through the plant and the human being, leads to a transformation of the previous imagination: the pure green sap becomes red, and this now pure red stream of life brings forth the red blossom of the rose. The entire inner process, with its sequential stages of contemplation and image-forming, flows into the image of the red rose, imbuing it with a meaningfulness that has its roots in my own, inner, spiritual activity.

If you are able to remain inside the soul space that opens as you progress, you find yourself immersed in a realm of living thought-pictures. They do not leave you cold. A complex blend of feelings accompany them. Let these feelings fill you. Live into the fine, flowing interplay of thought and feeling.

The final step lies in the forming of a new image, that of a black cross with seven bright red roses encircling its center. This is a symbolic image of the transformative gesture that lies in the interplay between contemplative thought and imagination in the path described above. This symbol can now become the focus of one's meditation. The image that you call back is a fully personalized symbolic image. Woven into it are the threads of your own thought activity, your own powers of imagination. It is yours, and yet it is more than yours. When you call it forth from your memory, it comes cloaked in the warmth and pleasure you might feel when thinking of an absent friend. Like a true friend, it can lead you into places you were unable to go alone.

The intentional interplay of contemplative thought and imagination is an essential aspect of the meditative path described by Rudolf Steiner. It leads the powers of thought from the cold, clear realms of the intellect into the warm expanses of the soul, where we experience human feeling and human will. The warmth frees thinking from the bonds of categorical rigidity; the light of thinking illuminates the human soul. Will, feeling and thought flow together in a new, fluid, mobile, creative unity.

Point and Periphery

The inner picture of the rose cross, crafted imaginatively through the process we have explored above is a mental image that has no direct connection to the sense-world. It derives its meaning from the inner activity of the thinking, feeling soul. This activity flows into it, as it were, and comes to rest. When we call the image back in meditation, it re-awakens the soul to the activity in which it was immersed when crafting the image.

In 1924, when speaking with a group of curative educators, Rudolf Steiner developed another form of symbolic or *Sinnbild* meditation. He spoke of this in conjunction with the morning and evening meditations mentioned at the beginning of this chapter: *I am in God* and *In me is God.* On a blackboard, he drew two figures, one above the other. The upper one consisted of a blue circle with a yellow point in the center; the lower one of a yellow circle with a blue point in the center. The blue circle with the yellow centerpoint accompanies the evening experience of, *In me is God;* the yellow circle with the blue centerpoint accompanies the morning experience, *I am in God.* The blue corresponds to "I" or "me"; the yellow to "God." In the evening, I picture the blue circle with the yellow centerpoint in conjunction with the mantric sentence, *In me is God;* in the morning, I picture the yellow circle with the blue centerpoint in conjunction with the sentence, *I am in God.*

As was mentioned above, Rudolf Steiner introduced this meditation when working with a small group of individuals, who had chosen to work with children in need of special care. It comes toward the end of a series of talks concerning developmental differences and morphological gestures of various aspects of the human body. One of these has to do with the polarity of form that can be recognized in the human head as opposed to the limbs: the head, with its structurally rigid, spherical shape, bears its center within; the limbs, with their mobile, articulated form, describe a peripheral expanse that Steiner speaks of as an inverted sphere centered in infinity. With this specific group of individuals, the meditation is thus placed within the context of their socio-cultural striving; it becomes a vocational meditation shared by a circle of people. In this sense, it becomes the meditative seed of a lived group meditation—the shared practice of caring for and educating the children whose destinies have brought them together with this group of teachers.

The next day, Steiner returns to the meditation and takes it a step further. He speaks of it explicitly in relation to the polar morphological gestures of the head and the limbs and he brings it into motion. He speaks of how you can let the circle and the point move towards one another, the blue point expanding to become the yellow circle, the blue circle contracting to the yellow point, then letting the transformation continue, one into the other, again and again. Point and circle become one vibrant rhythmic movement in the soul, an inner organic metamorphosis of form and color.

How different this experience is than that of the rose cross. The rose cross, with its austere clarity and stillness, stands within the soul as the symbolic presence of the inner activity that led to up to it. It takes the soul back into that activity. The metamorphosis of point and periphery leads the soul into something new. The living, dynamic mobility of form, the vibrant play of color, the paradoxical harmony between the forces of concentration and receptivity—the soul gestures of point and periphery—open deep reservoirs of strength and vitality. When I meditate on the rose cross, I experience the stirring of a seed within the soul, and a living imagination of the path of the soul's becoming, a path towards selfless innocence, fills my heart. The dynamic nature of the fluid transformation of the experienced point and the experienced circle fills me completely, weaving the entire expanse of the soul into a single vessel of intentionally engaged receptivity. Point and periphery—the two poles of the experienced self—become one.

In a rare aside, Rudolf Steiner, when presenting this meditation, mentioned one of the great challenges of modern meditation: persuading yourself that you are meditating without really doing it. Anthroposophical meditative practices rest on an intentional re-directing of the imaginative forces through which we form our mental images of the world. We don't usually notice these forces. They are at work, as it were, backstage. The mental image is what normally captures our attention, not the sculptural activity through which it is formed. Meditative practice only begins to bear fruit when we are able to immerse ourselves in the activity itself and the forces shaping it. We must come to know ourselves as painters rather than pictures, but not be satisfied to merely picture ourselves as painters or artists without entering into the process of creation. If our meditation rests on a picture of ourselves as meditants, we can perhaps feel good about ourselves because we are "doing" our meditations, but we will never come to anything in meditating that leads us, in fact, beyond ourselves.

The meditative practice that Steiner describes rests initially on being able to shift one's consciousness from a passive picturing to an intentional imaging, a shift from a picture consciousness to an imaginative consciousness. The process described in the rose cross meditation culminates in an imaginary touchstone, which calls forth a memory of its formative origin: it is a symbol born of intentional imaging with no exact counterpart in the sense world. It belongs to the soul world. In the experienced mobility of the metamorphosis of point and periphery, the forces through which an image is formed are no longer a memory but a living presence in the soul.

If I take into account my own experiences and what I have heard from others, taking hold of the forces of inner imaging is something that for many people does not come easily. It is easier to imagine and hold a point before the eye of the soul than it is to do so with a circle. The initial images are pale, the colors wan. The movement from one to the other occurs in a series of discrete steps with the forms jumping from one to the other. It can be quite frustrating. The harder you try to "see" something, the less likely you are to do so. The more you try to make the pictured forms metamorphose one into the other, the less likely they are to do so. In developing this capacity of soul, the visualization exercises mentioned at the beginning of this chapter can be a great help. These re-picturing exercises, in which we allow our powers of imagining to be guided by the lawfulness of living organisms, bring both substantiality and flexibility into the art of imagining. Forms become stronger and more resilient, colors grow to be more vibrant, imagined movements more fluid. Through practice, you also become aware of the inner shifts of focus that are necessary as you proceed. Form, color, and movement are born of different regions of the soul. The imaginative act draws on all of them.

Vocational Meditation

Beginning in 1919, Rudolf Steiner turned his attention to specific cultural or professional activities. He gave courses for teachers, curative educators, doctors, farmers, actors, and priests, as well as for university students. These courses mark a turning point in the development of anthroposophy. Steiner's work became a source of inspiration for cultural renewal and transformation.

Today, many people find their way to anthroposophy through the work that arose from these initial courses. I am no exception. I met anthroposophy initially through the work Rudolf Steiner did with the teachers at the first Waldorf school. The example of a vocational meditation I would like to explore more closely here is one that was given to these teachers following Rudolf Steiner's last talk to the faculty in October 1923. It came at the end of a series of three lectures in which he presented the battle of the archangel Michael with the dragon, and how this relates to modern education. He spoke explicitly about this only at the end of the final lecture, and after speaking of the nature of a Michaelic impulse in education, went on to say that he would bring this the next day in a condensed version for their meditations. The next day, he gave the teachers a meditation in the form of a mantric verse:

Spirit awareness,
Turn your gaze inwards;
Heart-felt touching
Rest upon tender soul being;
In prescient spirit awareness,
In heart-warm soul touching,
Is woven conscious-being.
Conscious-being, that from the above
and the below of human
existence
Binds cosmic light
To earthly darkness.

Spirit awareness
Heartfelt touching
Behold and touch
Within the human being
Weaving cosmic lightness
In reigning earthly darkness:
My own
Human formative force
Engendering
Power creating
Will bearing
Self.

And in the original German:

Geistiges Blicken,
Wende dich schauend nach innen;
Herzliches Tasten
Rühre am zarten Seelen-Sein;
Im ahnenden Geistes-Blicken,
Im herzhaften Seelen-Tasten,
Da webt sich Bewusst-Sein.
Bewusst-Sein, das aus dem Oben
Und dem Unten des Menschen-
Wesens
Bindet Welten-Helle
An das Erden-Dunkel.

Geistiges Blicken
Herzliches Tasten
Erblicke, Ertaste
Im Menschen-Innern
Webende Welten-Helle
In waltendem Erdendunkel:
Mein eigenes
Menschen-Bilde-Kraft
Zeugendes
Krafterschaffendes
Willentragendes
Selbst.

A mantric verse is meditative content clothed in language. The path of the meditant leads through the layers of experience present in language to an encounter with the creative presence in which it originates. Mantra or mantram is an ancient Sanskrit word meaning, literally, a tool or instrument of thinking. The immersion of consciousness in mantric repetition helps free it from the limitations imposed initially by our awareness of the sense world and lead it into a space of emptiness in which it can participate in the pure light and warmth of divine creativity. The mantram is a bridge from the earthly to the divine, from form to spirit, from a world of discrete objects to one of pure movement. By immersing itself in the sounds, words and meaning of the mantram, the seeking soul both creates and crosses the bridge.

Each mantram sensitizes or creates within the soul an attunement or familiarity with certain qualities of the divine. By returning to the mantram repeatedly over a period of time, the soul opens space within itself for these qualities of divine activity. The presence of the divine within the soul transforms and strengthens it. Meditative immersion becomes a source of never-ceasing strength for the challenges that await us in the world.

This meditation given above captures the creative essence of the thoughts Rudolf Steiner shared with the teachers during the three lectures mentioned above. At the time, the school was going through a challenging period. Things were not going well. Enthusiasm for the work was lagging; the demands of the final exams were making themselves felt throughout the school; the mood in the classrooms was heavy. In his talks, Steiner met this challenge head on and laid the foundation for a new educational culture, a shared striving based on enthusism and responsibility rooted in a spiritual understanding of the healing nature of the learning process. In each of the three talks, he returns to the necessity of achieving a living thinking, a thinking imbued with the rejuvenating forces of spiritual activity.

The talks culminate in a depiction of Mahatma Gandhi as the model for the quality of social consciousness needed by the teachers to find a healthy relationship to the pressures of modern civilization and finally in a contemplation of the archangel Michael's battle with the dragon. Here Steiner speaks again of the deadening affect intellectual thought has on the human soul and of the Michaelic challenge facing the teacher.

Throughout the three lectures, which contain some of the most complex explorations of the physiological alchemy of learning to be found anywhere in Rudolf Steiner's work, we meet again and again the transformative presence of the human I, or in the context of its earthly existence, the human self.

The meditation, which he brought the next day, is one that can lead to a real encounter with the I as the source of transformative creativity and moral conviction.

The meditation comes in the form of a verse with two stanzas. The first stanza consists of eleven lines; the second of twelve. They are given in free verse. The original German text has a repetitive end rhyme that occurs in the first nine lines. The last two lines of the first stanza almost rhyme. The second passage is more complex, less repetitive.

Similar observations can be made about the rhythm and alliterative characteristics of the original text. These are not present in the translation, a challenge we face with all of Steiner's mantric work, which deserves a fuller exploration than is possible here. Suffice it to say that in most translations either the poetic qualities are lost in the attempt to remain true to the content of the mantram or, vice-versa, the content takes on other nuances when one tries to recreate the poetic characteristics.

Keeping in mind the original significance of the term *mantra*—a tool to focus consciousness—we can ask in what way does this verse focus our thinking or, perhaps better, lead our consciousness?

There are two gestures that continue through both stanzas, and a third that appears in the first stanza and in which the second stanza culminates. Both passages begin with imperatives. The first is more gentle, the second stronger, more focused. Following the first imperative, we find ourselves in a complex tapestry of interwoven polarities, through which the shuttle of consciousness flies, binding one to another. Each line is rich with imaginative language. The nouns are alive, instances of activity personified.

Spirit-awareness, heart-felt touching—perhaps one could say the light and warmth of consciousness—in their intertwining in conscious-being, they bring the pure light of spirit-born idealism into the realm in which it can take shape in action and bear earthly fruit.

The lines of the second stanza are shorter, more compact.

We can feel the strength concentrated in them. When we live into these lines, letting them resonate through the soul, a soul attuned by the contemplative journey of the first stanza, we can feel the strength that pulses through them. And in this pulsing, weaving wellspring of vitality and strength, we find the source of our own being, each one of us.

Working with this meditation leads to an intimate, unveiled encounter with what Steiner, in another setting, would characterize as the "I" of the "inner night,"[40] the peripheral I: the nonconscious I of the will. It is the I from which flows forth the strength that enables us to live our higher ideals, to plunge through the skewed reflections of convention and stand true to the truth in any given situation. It is the source of that elusive presence we call authenticity. And it is where we as teachers find the sources of imagination and inspiration that enable us to spark and nurture the learning will of our students.

Rudolf Steiner gave no specific instructions concerning this meditation. He appears, however, to have hoped that all the teachers would work with it, each in his or her own way. Based on my own experiences with this meditation, I would venture the following remarks.

It is good to begin by learning the mantram by heart. The sooner you are free of the written word, the better. In the beginning, you can repeat the whole verse to yourself, either aloud or in silence. Speaking it aloud is often helpful. When speaking aloud, do so slowly and with feeling. The

40　Rudolf Steiner, *Psychologische Aphorismen*, p. 18

same holds true when working through the verse in silence. Go slowly enough that your soul—your "inner" life—has time to resonate and move with each word and phrase. Let them focus your consciousness. As your soul follows the path laid out by the verse, it will at times stumble over riddles; questions will arise. Let them. Notice them, linger and move on. Do the same with the sudden flashes of insight that occur when you have worked with the verse for a time. Notice them, linger a moment and move on. Let nothing distract you. Let nothing lead you astray.

Simone Weil, the young French philosopher and activist who Albert Camus described as "the only great spirit of our time," wrote about this practice in her "Spiritual Autobiography." She writes of a period in her life when she was picking grapes with laborers in the vineyards. A friend had introduced her to Greek, and she had decided to learn the Lord's Prayer by heart in that language:

> The infinite sweetness of this Greek text so took hold of me that for several days I could not stop myself from saying it over all the time...Since that time I have made a practice of saying it through once each morning with absolute attention. If during the recitation my attention wanders or goes to sleep, in the minutest degree, I begin again until I have once succeeded in going through it with absolutely pure attention.[41]

The practice proves to be surprisingly powerful. She

---

41   Simone Weil, *Waiting for God*, p. 72

experiences her thoughts being taken away from her body and transported to a place beyond the limitations of space.

> ...filling every part of this infinity of infinity, there is silence, a silence which is not an absence of sound but which is the object of a positive sensation, more positive than that of sound. Noises, if there are any, only reach me after crossing this silence.[42]

Give your attention fully and innocently to the verse. Let it lead you into the space beyond space, the silence beyond the lack of sound. Let it fill you with joy and strength for what the world asks of you.

The meditative experience of this verse is intensified by a contemplative study of its content. In my experience this is true of all Rudolf Steiner's mantric work. Study enriches and broadens one's relationship to the ideas and meanings contained in the verse. It is also possible to deepen this through imaginative and artistic explorations of the verse's meaning. Everything I can do to help my soul become more responsive to the qualities of spiritual experience living through the words of the verse helps. Engaging in contemplative dialogue with others working with the verse can be very helpful and stimulating. Each of us has his or her own way of looking at things. Seeing the same thing through another's eyes opens aspects of it to which we were perhaps blind before. I have worked with this meditation for many years, yet in every conversation, in every shared exploration, I discover something new.

---

42   Ibid.

This is also true each time I return alone to the meditation. In the beginning there were big "a-ha" moments as the meaning of each line became clear and the meditation as a whole began to make sense. Later on the discoveries became finer, more delicate—nuances of phrases, the sound of a word, breaks in the rhythm. (And now I find myself on the verge of sharing things about my relationship to this meditation that I didn't plan to. I am going to do so, and ask you, the reader, to be aware that I am digressing. It will be a short excursion.) With time, I found myself becoming fond of the verse, fond in the way one might feel about a friend. I began to care for it. It became important to me. For some years now, it has never been far from my side. When teaching or working with a school, I return to it as a meditative practice every morning. But sometimes, during the course of the day I will become aware of its presence—a gentle, steadying, joyous presence. In those moments, I am grateful for the opportunity to teach.

I believe that it is important here to note again that Rudolf Steiner gave this meditation to the teachers of the first Waldorf school. It is a professional or vocational meditation. The path it leads you is specific to the inner and outer challenges a teacher meets. The verse itself, the mantram, is thus only one part of the meditation or, one could say, the meditation of the mantram is one part of a greater whole. This has three parts—the work towards an increasingly insightful spiritual understanding of the child; the meditative transformation of this understanding through the work with the mantram; and the authentic creative practice of this understanding in the teacher's meeting with the growing child. These three practices are in fact one: they comprise the life of the modern, spiritually engaged, socially conscious teacher. Study and experience flow together in the act of meditation; from the meditative experience, insight and strength flow into the classroom and a sense of "groundedness" pervades further study.

Toward the end of his life, Rudolf Steiner spoke about this threefold relationship between contemplative study, meditative deepening, and cultural action in a number of different contexts. They all share one thing. In each case, Rudolf Steiner was speaking of the need to bring the spiritual insight gained through meditative practice selflessly to bear on the everyday realities of modern life.

XI. In Dialogue with Life: Practicing Anthroposophy

> But a person, I would say, is an individual living really
> with the world. And 'with' the world, I don't mean in the
> world—just in real contact, in real reciprocity with the
> world in all the points in which the world can meet man.
>
> Martin Buber

Years ago, when Max posed the question as to the nature of anthroposophical practice, all I could do was to describe my own practice—meditation, study, and responding freely to what the world asked of me. Was it right to portray this as the practice of anthroposophy? I shared my reservations with the circle at the time. They understood. Any modern spiritual practice will be given a specific or unique character by the individual practitioner. It is the nature of our time. The only true source of spiritual growth springs from the core of each individual. Once this stream begins to flow, the practice or practices one chooses serve to nurture but also to form it. Your practice shapes the path of your becoming.

Anthroposophy is often spoken about as a cognitive

path of inner schooling, as a path of knowledge. Perhaps it would be more appropriate to think of it as a path of understanding. The one-sided focus on the act of knowing does not capture the way what we know and how we come to know it affects the way we live our lives. True understanding arises when something we have come to know touches or moves us. Understanding always has an emotional component. Only when this happens does knowledge have the possibility of taking on meaning, to become knowledge that lives on and grows with us. To paraphrase Steiner: only then does what we grasp in the head stir the heart and radiate out into the will. Knowledge becomes understanding becomes deed. Thinking, feeling, and willing flow together to become the emergent expression of the evolving self.

Thus anthroposophy is neither a spiritual philosophy, mystical experience, nor religion. It is what comes to expression when these three realms of experience merge to form a new unity. Anthroposophy is a way of life. It is to be lived and practiced. With time, practice and life become one. You find yourself meeting the world with a calm, receptive mindfulness. New vistas open, drawing you onward along what is now your own path towards freedom. Becoming increasingly able to embrace fully the responsibilities that accompany freedom becomes the star by which you navigate.

Today when asked about the practice of anthroposophy I am less at a loss for words than I was 14 years ago. I often respond initially with the story of Zusya, one of the aphoristic sayings of the Hasidim collected by Martin Buber. It goes like this: A rabbi named Zusya died and went to stand before the judgment seat of God. As he waited for God to appear, he grew nervous thinking about his life and how little he had done. He began to imagine that God was going to ask him, "Why weren't you Moses or why weren't you Solomon or why weren't you David?" But when God appeared, the rabbi was surprised. God simply asked, "Why weren't you Zusya?"

The practice of anthroposophy rests upon this question, which forms, one might say, the cultural context within which anthroposophy finds its roots. Instead of the Old Testamentary "why weren't you…?", however, anthroposophy poses the question positively: "What does it take to become 'Zusya'?" The path described by Rudolf Steiner, with all its many facets and possibilities, is the path of Zusya becoming Zusya.

There is no such thing as general or abstract individuality. Each human being is on a path to becoming him- or herself. The future depends on this. All forms of collective beliefs, practices and morality become, at a certain point, hindrances in this process. The healing transformation of human society will not come about based on a collective consciousness. It will arise out of the actions of individuals who give of themselves freely and are able to recognize one another's gifts.

Goodness cannot be legislated. It flows forth from an individual when an idea is so permeated by love that it flows forth into the world as action. Anthroposophy, in as much as it is a spiritual practice, belongs to this moment in the evolution of human consciousness when the human I emerges from the cradle of traditional culture to become, as Herder put it, "the first to be released by creation." Thus, at the center of any anthroposophical practice is to be found the human I making its painful, joyous, courageous journey from selfishness to selfless/selfullness.[43] It is a path that transforms the radical philosophical individualism of the late nineteenth and early twentieth century into something more far-reaching and radical, though in a different sense. It leads through the morass of confusion, disenchantment, and alienation to which the I awakens when "submerged in materialism," to the experience of self that knows itself to be an essential part of a greater whole. Thus Rudolf Steiner's anthroposophy is markedly free of anything that could be construed as a collective belief system or as general rules of moral conduct. The path of the individual is an individual path.[44]

This is the first fundamental tenet of anthroposophical practice. It is a path of individual freedom. This freedom should not, however, be confused with license. The artist is free only when he or she has mastered craft and technique.

---

43   The latter is a word we unfortunately don't have in the English language. In this context it connotes an overflowing of the creative, empathetic, compassionate forces of the I, now free from any attachment to bodily or societal security. It describes a state of being in which the self awakens to and fully embraces its unity with the cosmos, without losing itself.

44   No form of suggestive visualization or group meditation that violates this basic tenet can be considered "anthroposophical."

The anthroposophical path rests on specific techniques or disciplines.

The first has to do with the unique nature of its point of departure: the transformation and spiritualization of thinking, accompanied by specific practices that help shift the way you respond to the "outside" world. These are practices of concentration, on the one side, and of receptivity on the other. They go hand in hand.

At all stages along the path of self-development described in Steiner's work, it is important to remain conscious of these two realms of experience. Whatever steps you take in one realm must be balanced by corresponding steps taken in the other. The depth of insight gained through all the practices related to the transformation of thinking requires of you ever-deepening reserves of compassion and self-lessness. Awakening the spiritualized forces of thinking is a powerful process of transformation. It can easily lead to feelings of arrogance and superiority, which can only bring good when borne into action on the more powerful forces of love.

The challenge of transforming and spiritualizing the capacity of thinking stands not only at the beginning of the anthroposophical path, it is a challenge that will continue to present itself at every point along the way. We always struggle, for instance, with the tendency to see the world through the eyes of what we have come to know. In this regard, knowledge that arises from anthroposophical or other spiritual sources can have the same limiting effect on our inner growth, as does knowledge derived from a positivist point of view. The dogmatic anthroposophist has the same possessive relationship to his ideas, as does the ideological scientist.

Just as the Buddhist path requires us to rid ourselves of attachments to worldly things, the anthroposophical path brings us to the point at which we must rid ourselves of attachments to the things of the mind: Learn in each moment to see the world with eyes unclouded and free of prejudice, not artificially focused by pre-conceived notions. In tomorrow's world, wonder is of much more value than analytical acuity.

As you begin to master practices of attentiveness in these two realms of experience, what lies between them begins to take on new significance. A new dimension of the path becomes apparent; another realm of practice opens before you. At its core is the most human of all capacities: the capacity of imagination. The next level of practice lies in the mastery of the forces of imagination or, in the words of Samuel Taylor Coleridge, "the living Power and prime Agent of all human perception, [the] repetition in the finite mind of the eternal act of creation in the infinite I AM."

By mastering the forces of imagination you intentionally open your soul to what lives in the world around you. The experience of certain emotional states, like compassion and reverence, are impossible without a corresponding depth of imaginative experience. Only by honing and objectifying your capacity for imagination can you make space within your consciousness for those aspects of the world that are present, yet not seen. You learn to stand among the things you experience instead of merely gazing out at them. This is the true mystery of understanding, of standing or living with the things, rather than experiencing them as apart from you. You become aware of the intangible qualities at work in the world, those that weave in, through, and between all that surrounds you. The world speaks within you and the more capable you become in hearing what it has to say, the more strongly you come to know yourself as a creative participant in the true nature of its becoming.

The third stage of practice takes on form when you bring the forces of attentiveness and imagination to bear on a specific task in life, when you place your awakening capacities in service to the earth, to nature, or to your fellow human beings. Anthroposophy culminates, and finds its validity, in what Heinz Zimmermann termed "evolutionary revolution." Without the individual's commitment to bring the fruits of his or her transformation and growth to bear on the socio-cultural challenges of the time, anthroposophy runs the risk of losing its vital connection to the karmic forces of reality in the world. When the revolutionary impulse becomes trapped in the self-serving limitations of a middle-class mentality it severs itself from its own source of constant renewal.

This sets anthroposophy, as a practice, apart from other schools of spiritual development. The source of its vitality lies in the future, in the blossoming of the nascent seeds in the human soul. It is a spiritual path rooted in the future, in what is in the process of becoming. Adopting its practices as an individual path means to free oneself from the past, thus becoming able to stand freely in the present. Only when one is present does the present moment cease to be but a fleeting passing. Only by learning to be present can I become a responsible co-creator in the great unfolding of the cosmos.

Bibliography

Owen Barfield, *Poetic Diction: A Study in Meaning*. Oxford: Barfield Press, 2010.

Samuel Taylor Coleridge, *Biographia Literaria: The Collected Works of Samuel Taylor Coleridge, Biographical Sketches of my Literary Life and Opinions*. Princeton: Princeton UP, 1983.

Karl-Martin Dietz, et al, *Rudolf Steiners 'Philosophie der Freiheit': Eine Menschenkunde des hoeheren Selbst*, Stuttgart: Freies Geisteleben, 1994.

Maurice Merleau-Ponty, *Phenomenology of Perception*. London: Routledge, 2012.

Sten Nadolny, *The Discovery of Slowness*. Philadelphia: Paul Dry Books, 2005.

Edward S. Reed, *From Soul to Mind: The Emergence of Psychology from Erasmus Darwin to William James*. New Haven: Yale University Press, 1997.

Malidoma Patrice Somé, *Of Water and the Spirit: Ritual, Magic and Initiation in the Life of an African Shaman*, Penguin Compass, 1994.

Rudolf Steiner, *Anthroposophical Leading Thoughts*. London: Rudolf Steiner Press, 1998.

——, *Anthroposophy: An Introduction*. London: Rudolf Steiner Press, 1983.

——, *Aphorismen*. Dornach: Rudolf Steiner Verlag, 1971.

———, *Autobiography: Chapters in the Course of My Life, 1861–1907 (CW 28)*. Great Barrington: SteinerBooks, 2000.

———, *Briefe Band II: 1890-1925 (GA 39)*. Dornach: Rudolf Steiner Verlag, 1987.

———, *Education for Special Needs: The Curative Education Course (CW 317)*. Forest Row: Rudolf Steiner Press, 2014.

———, *Guidance in Esoteric Training*. London: Rudolf Steiner Press, 2001.

———, *How to Know Higher Worlds*. Great Barrington: Anthroposophic Press, 1994.

———, *An Outline of Occult Science*, Anthroposophic Press, 1939.

———, *The Philosophy of Freedom*. London: Rudolf Steiner Press, 1979.

———, *Die Rätsel der Philosophie (GA 18)*. Dornach: Rudolf Steiner Verlag, 1985.

———, *Study of Man: General Education Course*. London: Rudolf Steiner Press, 2004.

———, *Die Welt der Sinne und die Welt des Geistes (GA 134)*. Rudolf Steiner Verlag, 1990.

———, *The World of the Senses and the World of the Spirit (CW 134)*. Forest Row: Rudolf Steiner Press, 2014.

Andreas Suchantke, *Metamorphosis: Evolution in Action*. Ghent, NY: Adonis Press, 2009.

Shunryu Suzuki, *Zen Mind, Beginner's Mind*. Boston: Shambahla, 2011.

Simone Weil, *Waiting for God,* Harper and Row, 1973.